Overlander

*Bikepacking coast to coast
across the heart of the Highlands*

Alan Brown

Saraband

Published by Saraband,
Digital World Centre,
1 Lowry Plaza,
The Quays, Salford, M50 3UB
and
Suite 202, 98 Woodlands Road,
Glasgow, G3 6HB
www.saraband.net

ISBN: 9781912235414
ebook: 9781912235421

Printed and bound in Great Britain by Clays Ltd, Elcograf S.p.A.

10 9 8 7 6 5 4 3 2 1

*Every effort has been made to ensure that the information contained in this book is
correct. Details about land and estate owners come from the Registers of Scotland,
Companies House, and other sources, and are accurate to the best knowledge of the
author and publisher at the time of printing. The author and publisher make no
claim that the route as described here is safe for cyclists: it is accessible under the Land
Reform Act 2003, but anyone wishing to recreate the route does so at their own risk.*

Maps © 2019 Saraband. Overall Scotland source map © d-maps.com

"*Overl* .... preciousness
of the .... ry cycling to
what it should be ... Alan Brown traces a new/old Scotland through
a network of coffin paths, estate tracks, drove roads, military roads,
disused railway beds and sheer bog. It's an uplifting account ...
A very timely reminder that inactivity and loss of contact with nature
... er threats than most small accidents." *Lesley Riddoch*

... ling and walking are the best ways of truly appreciating a place.
...lander, Alan Brown has written a hugely readable account
... at he hears, sees, smells and thinks of the present and the
... . Sensitive, personal and culturally informed ... an eloquent
... der of the wonderful country we live in ... Time to get on my
... " *ndy Wightman MSP*

"Riding a bike across Scotland's byways offers endless possibilities
... ploration, adventure and fun and most importantly, offers
... pportunity to read the small print of our highland landscape.
...nder is a remarkable book, the tale of a strenuous mini-
... re and a clarion call to those who manage our upland areas."
... *on McNeish*

« Heureux qui loin des cours, dans un lieu solitaire,
Se prescrit à soi-même un exil volontaire,
Et qui, lorsque Zéphire a soufflé sur les bois… »

Edmond Rostand, *Cyrano de Bergerac* (1897)

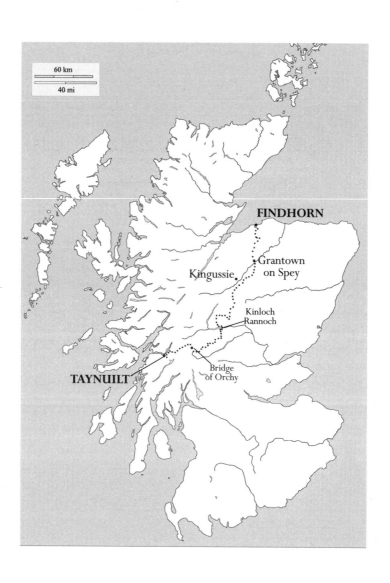

Contents

Introduction

It was only with many years of hindsight that I understood I'd fallen in love the first time I rode a bicycle. That's how it goes with me: always the last to know what my own heart had been up to decades before. It was the feeling of freedom, the sense of independence that thrilled me. Many of us can remember the first time we took off on a bike without a helping hand or stabilisers; the giddy exhilaration of realising that you're actually doing it, flying at an unprecedented rate by your own minimal efforts. In my case it was a summer evening in Aberdeen's Desswood Place and someone – I can't remember who – pulled the old trick of saying they were holding the saddle and then letting go once I was up to speed. My childish mind knew at once that this sensation was important and I grabbed hold of it, banking the confidence and capacity that came with this first step into the grown-up world.

Once I'd felt the queer sensation of an object as uncooperative as a bicycle apparently obeying my orders, there was never any turning back. I can't remember much about my first bike except that it was second-hand, carefully repainted in bright colours by my old man, and had white balloon tyres. Before long I was bombing around the pavements and lanes with my brother and his pals. Being able to ride a bike was probably the single most liberating thing to learn after speech. Everyday access to the sensation of speed and the annihilation of distance are not trivial things even for adults, let alone small children. It's really something that should be celebrated by a joyful and profound coming-of-age ceremony for all of us, marking our mastery of possibly the most useful and benign tool humans have ever invented.

But back then, instead of a celebration, we were subjected to the infamous cycling proficiency process, designed to convince any child that they would be instantly killed if they attempted to cycle on a main road and immediately arrested if they ventured out with a slack chain or soft tyres. The triangular, enamelled cycling proficiency badge that we all received at the end of the indoctrination has since become a byword amongst my generation for a useless qualification handed out to all and sundry, and rightly so. At the point where I could have been getting myself to school and back, I basically stopped cycling, even as my best friend at secondary school was pretty much independently inventing mountain biking by taking his mum's sturdy old shopping bike into the Cairngorms to shorten the approach to the more distant peaks.

I don't know what it was that made me buy a bike as a student in Edinburgh. Maybe it was just that at the age of twenty I was getting over myself a bit and didn't mind doing something less than super-cool, or maybe I was simply tired of walking everywhere. I got myself a British-made touring bike with drop handlebars from a shop in Rodney Street, down in Canonmills, at a time when I lived in Marchmont. I can still recall the sense of disbelief at the steepness of the road back up to Princes Street and the speed of the thundering cars. The traffic has got steadily worse since, but my ability to treat it like it's part of a video game, rather than a stream of angry metal, is now near perfect. I seriously believe you'd go mad cycling in town these days if you really thought about what might be going on in the minds of the people directing a ton of steel just inches from your fragile skeleton.

That bike lasted me fourteen years and the only real change I made to it was to put on straight handlebars. I never could understand how you were supposed to see where you're going or use the brakes on bikes with drop bars. Also I seemed to need surgical intervention to unfold my liver after I'd been using one for any period of time, so uncomfortable was the riding position. Now a touring bike with flat bars on it is essentially a hybrid bike, something I wasn't even aware existed at that time. So I'm going to claim that I independently invented the hybrid – a bicycle with a mountain-bike riding position but more road-friendly tyres and gears. It's a type of bike that has interested me ever since, seeming to offer my cycling holy grail: one bike that will do everything, from the commute to work to a leisurely tour to a bit of light trail riding, though the manufacturers would have you believe that you need a different bike for every task. They sell a bewildering array of models, from cruisers to dirt bikes, from track bikes to road racers, from Audax bikes to gravel and cross bikes, from hipster fixies to folders to cargo bikes, and from roadsters to mountain bikes. But I reckon the spirit of cycling is for one bike to do most of what you need.

When I'd eventually finished being a student and gone to work, I got to know a gentleman in the changing rooms who worked on the phones in our office. He was actually a millionaire who'd set up and sold one of the first ever call centres in England and retired north on the proceeds to concentrate on growing ornamental maples, but our employer knew nothing about that. He'd just come in to work out of boredom and bought himself a new bike for the commute, which he chained up on the railings outside. It was probably the first off-road-oriented hybrid I'd ever seen, with an alloy-frame, suspension fork and seat post, and tyres that fell halfway between the skinny slick things that roadsters use for speed and the craggy mud-pluggers that mountain bikers use for grip, and it got me to wondering exactly how much this one bicycle could do.

By this time, the steel frame of the bike I'd bought as a student had started to rust and it was time to pass it on to someone without a bike at all to get them cycling – in this case, a friend who'd hit fifteen stones, with no sign of that being his upper limit. When my first ever Christmas bonus hit the bank I was off down to the bike shop and bought myself the next model up in the range from my colleague's. It had the standard fittings for the turn of the century: V-brakes, steel-sprung suspension fork and seat post, and twenty-four gears. I fell in love with it immediately. The stiffness of the alloy frame (made of what were, back then at least, over-sized tubes) seemed to transmit every ounce of effort into the back wheel. And the suspension soaked up the bonus features of Edinburgh's tarmac so well that it allowed me to concentrate on the traffic rather than just staying upright.

While I never much got into the mountain biking craze that kicked off at the same time, I would sometimes ride my hybrid proudly over the Pentland Hills after work, just to tease the serious riders on their serious mountain bikes by cheerily greeting them as I passed by on a commuter bike. Mountain biking was, it seemed to me, becoming a sport concentrated in prepared trail centres where speed and technical mastery of obstacles encountered in a headlong downhill rush, combined with an encyclopaedic knowledge of the layout of the trails, were the whole object rather than incidental to the process. It's hard to deny the exhilaration of swooping through pine trees at forty miles an hour on a bicycle, but at the same time it's hard to deny just how insanely dangerous that is or how tightly your attention focuses on the path ahead when there's the prospect of taking a tree in the face.

Mountain biking was invented by a bunch of free-spirited Californians looking for ways to access the hills behind their coastal towns. They built a lot of their bikes from scratch or based them on the cruiser bikes used for leisurely rides along the seafront. There was a definite counter-cultural and meditative aspect to the practice, an attempt to engage with the landscape and the process of designing and making things. But their gentle, wide-ranging, artisanal pastime seems to have become a medium of competition, speed and consumption focused on a few playparks. How did a practice that was born on bikes home-brewed by eccentrics become a sport dominated by machines costing several thousand pounds transported by car to carefully curated walled gardens?

My take on the whole thing changed when I came across Phil McKane's classic book about the wild trails of the Highlands and Lowlands that weren't designed to be crossed by bike but that you *can* cycle on (see bibliography). While most of the rides it describes are loops to be carried out in a day or an afternoon, what really caught my eye was the bonus section at the back that detailed a multi-day, coast-to-coast expedition from Fort William to Montrose. I got to wondering if I was capable of riding the route on my ageing hybrid, with the minimal changes of putting some chunkier tyres on and a single-wheeled trailer to carry food and camping kit. In 2013, with the independence referendum looming and my mind not made up on the question in hand, it seemed like the right time to give it a go and, together with my oldest friend, we did just that. It was transformative in many ways, including a huge boost to my confidence. But the most beguiling thing was that when I arrived at the beach at St Cyrus, having traced a path across the country from one side to the other, I found I could traverse that line again entirely in my mind, taking in some wild, wonderful and historical places along the way. I was left with a new perspective on the country from the one that I had when I set out from the pier at Caol.

* * *

It was the sight of the red wax seal on the coffin that did it. I learnt early on when I worked in France that nothing — no matter how serious it might look — is official without the right stamp, and this was the right stamp. Or, the wrong stamp. This was very much the wrong stamp. Cécile was officially dead. She and I had worked together in chemistry half a lifetime ago. Our whole research group worked with a solvent linked to cancer — all except Cécile. She had only worked with water, but, by the cruel and arbitrary ways of the world, it was she who had found a lump in her back. And it was her in the coffin, and it was me in the suit.

Cécile was born to look after folk and to teach them. I still don't really know what it was that brought her to work in a research lab here, but my life is all the richer for it. She taught me that swimming can be fun, overcoming the best efforts of everyone else who had ever tried to teach me. When I went to work in her country she declined any further conversation in English and taught me that the beer-drinking student union bouncer I thought I knew was, in fact, a witty, gentle and utterly feminine French lady. She taught me the essential nature of France with nothing more than a couple of second-hand books from a market — a scabrous cartoon strip and the text of Rostand's play, *Cyrano de Bergerac*. I hadn't seen enough of her since I came back to Edinburgh, and I wouldn't be seeing any more of her, and it didn't seem right or fair. The world seemed threadbare and careworn.

It was the summer of 2016, a slippery, queasy time. Each day was a half-remembered hallucination as the country turned its back on forty years of fractious neighbourliness in a spasm of desperation and distrust. My first real political memory is of the European referendum in 1975, when I got a day off primary school and a trip in the car to the polling station with my dad. I asked him what was going on and once he'd told me he also revealed what choice he'd made. I asked him why, and his reply has stayed with me ever since.

'For you.'

The 2016 referendum felt very much like a conversation that was for someone else, some*where* else. There was nothing in it for people like me, who'd made friends like Cécile and later gone to work in her country without so much as a by-your-leave, although there had been a full day's traipsing round from one police station to another at the behest of various sardonic clerks. Now it looked like my country was to be cut off from its oldest friends and cata-pulted into a brave new location somewhere in the north Atlantic. I've never felt more distantly alien than when I dialled up the news on the screen each morning of that unreal time.

For the previous few years I'd worked as a contractor in a variety of Edinburgh's august institutions and counting houses. There are good and bad points to being a freelancer rather than an employee. The freedom to decide not to work is definitely one of the better ones. I'd planned to take that summer off after working in Stirling for a year, the first time I'd ever commuted to work by car. It had left me fatter, weaker and sadder than I'd ever been, despite the money. I've cycled to every single job I've had since I was a student and it's been a constant in my life through all weathers. It doesn't matter how menial your job is, a commute through Edinburgh is likely to be something you could sell as a tourist excursion, and the sculptural profile of the city keeps anyone on a bike fit. There's also a mysterious but undeniable effect on your mood from turning over the cranks of a bicycle outdoors, a feeling that somehow it is good and natural for a human being to be astride that most elegant of carriages.

So, that summer, three years on from my first overland ride, with both me and the nation paralysed by decision and indecision, I needed to look hard at myself – and the country – and to carve another line from sea to sea and across my own heart.

* * *

After bicycles, maps must be the best thing ever. I can happily spend an hour lost in Ordnance Survey (OS) maps, filter-feeding like a geographical whale in the sea of information. I can make whole journeys across the paper, reconstructing the terrain from the contour lines and the vegetation. There's an enormous dignity in the absolute unvarnished honesty that lets you deduce things that the cartographer never measured directly. I already knew from the McKane book of a ride that passed through Taynuilt, just up the west coast from Oban, and also that there was a rideable pass north through the Cairngorms from Atholl to Speyside. The question was whether I could link these to make a satisfying traverse from the south-west to the north-east, cutting through the classic coast-to-coast route to make a diagonal cross on the map.

It didn't take too long to find a way that was theoretically possible on a heavily loaded bike. The internet confirmed with video evidence that most of it had already been ridden by someone. In any case, as I'd already found out, no bit of terrain is impossible to cycle if you're willing to dismantle everything and carry it. Portage isn't much fun, but it can get you over the trickiest few hundred metres of a journey and, on the route I picked, the maps did seem to show a kilometre of trackless bog in the middle, but otherwise a feasible route from Taynuilt to Findhorn, twenty-five miles east of Inverness. The crowning glory was the almost total lack of public road in the whole route, with only forty kilometres of tarmac out of a total of two hundred and seventy.

From Taynuilt on the Atlantic coast, the idea was to go north up the east side of Loch Etive before turning inland at Glen Kinglass. Then over the first watershed to Inveroran and Glen Orchy for a small southwards backtrack before turning east up Glen Auch and over into Tayside in upper Glen Lyon. From Innerwick, an old coffin road leads over to Loch Rannoch, from where an ancient drove road goes to Dalnaspidal. A modern cycle path heads down to Dalnacardoch and the entry to the Gaick Pass through the Cairngorms to Glen Tromie on Speyside. From there, forest roads lead to Glen Feshie, Glen More and the Ryvoan Pass to Abernethy, where more logging roads lead to the Speyside Way, which in turn connects to the Dava Way, built on the bed of an old railway to Forres. Finally, a mix of public roads and cycle ways leads to Findhorn and the North Sea.

It's a journey through the meat of the nation, against the flow of all the modern transport links and spurning the obvious and much shorter parallel route up the Great Glen. I reckoned that whatever else I got from it, I'd learn something worth knowing about both myself and the country I was crossing. Modern travel so often seems like something we're subjected to and tolerate in a trance-like state, waiting to be delivered like parcels. This would be a proper expedition, requiring me to provide everything, from the planning and logistics to the motive power, and to deal with all the risks on the way. It would be a wilful retreat into another era when journeys could and did go wrong, in open defiance of a world where we all seem to be adrift in currents of someone else's making.

* * *

One thing I learned from the classic crossing was that my bike, though adequate, had been overwhelmed at times by the rigours of the trail. Part of my idea for that trip had been to prove to myself that the bike I rode to work every day would manage to cross the country with no changes other than off-road tyres – and it had done just that, but with a cost to my joints and adrenal glands. The gearing had been a bit too high, leaving my knees aching, and the suspension and brakes had struggled to cope with the descent off the Corrieyairick Pass, where the heavy trailer had been altogether too keen to come round and visit the front wheel. I had to admit there was a limit to what cheap commuting gear could do, but I was still oddly, passionately loyal to the frame itself and the idea that one bike can pretty much do everything.

The gearing problem was easily solved by fitting mountain bike chain rings on the front, giving me a lowest gear where one turn of the pedals would advance the bike about a metre and a half. On flat ground that feels ridiculously light, like the pedals aren't connected to anything, but on loose, steep climbs on a heavily loaded bike it allows you to progress at walking pace. Gearing lower than this is hard to achieve and leads to problems balancing because you're going so slowly.

The real problem had been the front suspension, which was a cheap unit meant to iron out the odd bump in urban tarmac; it had proved simply inadequate in the face of the wild trails. As a hybrid, my bike had the big, twenty-nine-inch wheels you get on road bikes rather than the twenty-six-inch ones on the original mountain bikes. For a long time no one made decent suspension forks for this size of wheel, but then marketing and fashion demanded a change to push new bike sales. The twenty-niner mountain bike was born. When an ex-demo air-sprung trekking fork of the right size came up in the New Year sales, it seemed daft not to jump at the chance to upgrade. All I was doing was putting the equipment onto the bike that it would have if it was developed today. This didn't seem like a breach of trust with the bike I'd bought, just part of the job of keeping it going as long as possible and totally in keeping with the spirit of its design.

Changing the fork also meant I had to change the front brake. The originals were cable-operated V-brakes, which, when properly adjusted, can be hugely powerful. But they do have the drawback that they operate on the rim of the wheel, which on this type of trip would often be covered in mud, sand or water. Hydraulic disc brakes have even more power and also more feel to them than any cable-operated brake. There's more feedback through the lever about what's going on where the friction material and the braking surface meet. Ultimately, I had no choice anyway as the new fork only had mounts for disc brakes, but the rear brakes were another matter.

I could have left the cable-operated rear brakes in place but it just seemed wrong to mix hydraulics with classic brakes. The frame, however, having been designed in the last century, had no mounts for disc brakes. The solution came one evening when I was getting my shopping after work. Chained up next to mine was the kind of practical commuter bike you can barely buy here: dynamo lights, full mudguards, hub gears and ... hydraulic *rim* brakes. An online search showed the bike was German, as I'd thought, and that the brakes in question were very highly regarded by continental commuters and trials riders the world over.

Putting the whole lot together gave me a quite unique machine. No one has yet been quite so cruel as to use the term Frankenbike, but the mechanics I knew would raise an eyebrow when they saw it. A late-nineties alloy hybrid frame with mountain bike gears, hydraulic rim brakes, hydraulic disc brakes, trekking tyres and a fancy-pants magnesium air-sprung short-travel fork; it made for what I would say is the most capable hybrid ever – and which others might just say is the world's worst twenty-nine-inch mountain bike.

I just think it's the way any human object should be: loved, used, repaired and improved. So many of the things we buy seem to spend only the most fleeting time in our hands before they head off to landfill, an idea that causes me nothing but despair. There are good quality jobs to be had in maintaining and repairing objects. You really need to understand any device to fix it, and even more so to adapt it. The culture of disposability, of using cheaply produced goods for a year or two before discarding them, has the effect of hollowing out the skills we need to not just make things but to keep them going. It's surely not something that can continue forever, requiring as it does the constant stoking of our thirst for novelty, our disdain for what was novel last year. My bike was fine sixteen years ago when I bought it and it'd do me fine now. The journey would be just as enjoyable as it would have been if I'd splashed out two grand for a brand new trekking bike, and probably even more enjoyable because I knew every bolt and every ball bearing of the machine I'd be riding. It may sound odd, but I've got a real relationship with this thing, even though I've never given it a name. Machines are to be used, not loved, and names are for people, for whom that rule is reversed.

So I have a journey to make and a faithful companion to make it with. I will ride my bike across the Grampian Mountains, from Taynuilt on the Atlantic coast to Findhorn on the Moray Firth, using the least amount of public road possible and carrying everything I need. I'll find water on the way and sleep in bothies when I can.

From the late medieval period until the mid-Victorian times there was a class of men – and it does seem to have been men – who moved cattle to market from the Highlands and Islands to the Lowlands over ancient routes through the hills, carrying oatmeal, onions and whisky with them and sleeping wrapped in the plaid. When the Disarming Acts came in after the Jacobite uprisings these drovers were specifically allowed to continue to carry arms, so rough were their lives and so dangerous their trade. They bore all of the financial and physical risks of their droves themselves, relying on guile and ingenuity if they were to return home with any profit. What I'm proposing to do pales into insignificance compared to what they did many times a year. I'll be going about four times as far each day as they did, but I'll have a variety of luxuries that they could only have dreamed of.

First, I'll have trails to follow and bridges across many of the rivers. Until the eighteenth century bridges were virtually unknown in the Highlands. The larger rivers like the Spey had ferry boats on them, though the drovers would often just swim or ford them in their upper, wilder reaches. They generally followed routes only approximately, the cattle's feet marking braided, complex ways that were never metalled and often stuck to high ground, whereas modern routes stay as low as possible. I'll have all manner of paths and tracks to follow, from estate roads to logging roads, the remains of the military roads, modern leisure paths and disused railways. Many of them will have seen drove traffic at one time or another but all of them will since have become much more practical means of communication.

I'll also have modern waterproof and cold-weather gear: a tent, fleeces, merino wool tops and a synthetic sleeping bag. I'll have a spirit stove to make hot food any time I want, while they might not have got anything warm for weeks at a time, except the blood drained from their living beasts (with the *sgian-fhala* bloodletting knife) and mixed with oatmeal. I'll have a mobile phone. And I'll have a bicycle. Perhaps the only common points are that the journey will be made entirely under my own steam and that solace will be taken in alcohol at the end of each day.

For an ageing office worker like me to choose to give up hot water and beds for a week, to grind across the uplands of his country on his own, counts as pretty eccentric; but, had it been remotely comprehensible, it would have been deemed luxury travel not so long ago. Yet despite this, it feels like an attempt to connect to those people who made their way across our landscape before the eras of mobility and then hyper-mobility that we know now, and to share a little bit of their hardship and sense of adventure. It's a manifestation of the human need to make pilgrimage, a journey with a goal that's more than just the destination, and to be tested physically and morally on the way. It feels absurd and unfair that my friend is dead and I'm alive, and the overbearing sense of national drift only deepens my sense of unease and bewilderment. What better salve for the hurt than to reach inside myself to see if I can confront and overcome obstacles in the landscape? What better way to reconcile myself than to lay my head on that same land each night to sleep?

One

Argyll

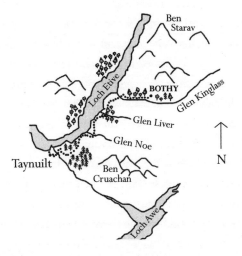

The natural way to travel to Taynuilt, and then back from Findhorn
a few days later, is by train. There are stations at Taynuilt and
Forres and that's partly why I chose the route in the first place.
It's well known that you can transport a bicycle on the rail network, but possibly less well known, certainly to me, that you can
no more take a bicycle trailer on a train than a piano, a kayak or
a hang glider. Rules are rules and no offer of extra payment is of
any interest, which leaves me with a logistical problem and the
need to confront my ideas of total self-reliance on this trip almost
immediately: I have to ask my partner, Nathalie, if she's willing
to drop me off in the car at one end and pick me up at the other.

She was already worried about me taking off into the hills on
my own and had only given her consent to the venture on the
understanding that she'd come and meet me halfway, where I cross

the main north–south road through the Highlands. I wonder if my offer for her to join me on the first day – for a ride up Loch Etive – might be worth a lift up to Taynuilt and back from Findhorn. After a bit of negotiation (and possibly a certain underplaying of the effort involved in bikepacking on my part), agreement is eventually reached and a date in mid-July set for the mission to be launched. As a French national who made her life here long before we met, she is in as much need of a *tête-à-tête* with her adopted country as me, so she agrees that she will pack her bike and ride with me up to Glen Kinglass before heading home the next morning as I head out into the known unknowns of the Grampians.

So on a fine afternoon in July I find myself mooching around the carpark of the small harbour at Taynuilt, which may well technically be in Bonawe or Brochroy. It's that kind of place – a few scattered hamlets on the flat ground where the River Awe runs into Loch Etive. To cope with the anxiety that comes so easily to me from setting out on a course that may end in failure, injury, or both, I tend to fuss and grump. I fiddle around and find things that seem important but which weren't on the original list of essentials.

One of those that actually *is* indispensable is the photo on the starting line. For a coast-to-coast journey, this shot has to have a maritime background and indicate the pensive but determined attitude of the rider. If you can't get one foot in the salt water for the shot then the next best thing is to do it on a convenient jetty, which means you actually start out a few metres into the sea. But there's no way I'm pushing the bike all the way to the end of the tumbledown pier for the photo, and I opt to ride along it instead. It's not the ideal place for a warm-up: the gigantic granite blocks that the pier is built of have sagged and settled and there's no railing or anything to prevent me from driving straight into the sea.

And once the fully loaded trailer is hitched up to the bike the first few metres of pedalling feel quite strange. The bike's longer than it was, heavier, and has a new articulation.

In front of the camera I select an expression and posture in the hope that, when I look back at the images, I'll have a chance of remembering what I felt like: slightly scared, a bit irritated that I didn't do this thirty years ago, and more than a little excited that I have almost no idea what's going to happen over the next week.

The pier is a favourite spot for tourists who fancy a bit of fishing and we're treated to a show of disinterest from a fat man in a Rangers top trying to hide the fact that his hook is snagged on the seabed and isn't coming back with or without a fish any time soon. Nathalie gets some suitably moody shots of me, for when I come to doubt I ever actually tried this. In turn, I get some more jovial photos of her and even manage to get the fisherman in the same shot as her pink cycling undershorts as she swings her leg over her bike. I built it for her from a frame I found when I was out running one day, the contents of a few friends' garages and spare parts from a local bike recycler. It needed repainting and Nathalie hummed and hawed over the colour and, after much badgering, eventually sighed, 'Oh I don't know – *bleu, blanc, rouge*.' And that's exactly what she got. An alloy mountain bike frame with a rigid fork, big fat road tyres and full mudguards; meant for commuting but quite able to cope with a bit of light trail riding and painted in the colours of the *Tricolore*. You'd think the Rangers guy would have appreciated a red, white and blue bike, but he may have sensed its essential un-Britishness.

The ride back from the jetty to the car park and on to the road allows for another couple of nervous checks before that fateful feeling of turning the cranks over for the first time in earnest on a long trip, the mixture of hope and apprehension that's accompanied everything worthwhile in my life. The first kilometre is on tarmac, with a sharp left turn at the church along the lane that leads to the footbridge over the River Awe. I don't know why but the fiddling and navigational confusion in the first hour of a trip often seems to be equal to the sum of all faff throughout the rest of the day. True to form, there's backtracking and general uncertainty as we make our way round the back of the historical Bonawe iron foundry. But after the last few days of heavy rain the holes in the rutted Land Rover track are filled with deep black water and it's good to get the bike dirty straight away, feeling the suspension iron out the potholes and the tyres grip in the unseen mud.

The easy way to cross the Awe is over the road bridge a few kilometres down the A85, but this trip isn't about the easy way to get anywhere. It doesn't take six days to cycle from here to Findhorn the easy way, so of course we're heading over the pedestrian bridge that leads straight across to Inverawe and the forest trails.

Before we reach the bridge we come to a gate and I enact, for the first time of many, the ceremony needed to get a bike and trailer through a five-bar gate together with any dignity. A bike on its own will fall if it's not propped up firmly, but a bike with a single-wheeled trailer will enter into a conspiracy with gravity not just to fall over but to curl itself up like a snake and drive the handlebars into your groin while it does it. Also, because of the extra length of the trailer, you can't just scoot through and let the gate drop shut behind you because all that happens is that the gate drops onto the trailer and you're left stuck. You can go back and free it but the whole thing will then promptly faint and fall over. This isn't an issue that's ever covered in adverts for mountain biking kit and it certainly isn't the most glamorous aspect of Highland bikepacking.

Once we get the bikes through the gate we're left at the top of a lovely water meadow looking across to the bridge. Any mountain biker worth their body armour would set off and plough photogenically through the marshy ground. I'm tempted to do the same – am I not a rough, tough mountain biker, after all? But just how deep is the swamp? What's in it? Will the trailer's small wheel make it through? Will I hit something hidden and dump myself over the handlebars into the water? If I do that, I might not get dry for days. The tension that will play out the whole way – between wanting to have fun and wanting to get to Findhorn in one piece – sees me pushing the bike through the morass as I tiptoe along the rotten planks laid by the locals. The boards sag under my weight and it's a close-run thing that my waterproof shoes aren't inundated. I've only two pairs of socks with me and I do not want to get the first pair wet after only half an hour, so I find myself walking *en pointe* like a ballerina. It feels like an important part of setting the tone for the week. No stupid risks, no showboating.

Back when the first serious maps were made of the country, the Awe was crossed by a ford, but today it looks like an Olympic kayak course with roiling, deep black water that an elephant would struggle to stay upright in. There's a cable-stayed suspension footbridge now and as I approach it I'm propelled sideways and hear that high-pitched cracking sound so characteristic of something hitting the thin plastic shell of a bicycle helmet. I'm so keen to get going that I've walked straight into the steel cable and, as is so often the case, my inadvertent movement is much better timed than my deliberate ones. I'm ricocheted back, feeling a phantom of the pain that would have resulted if I'd driven my naked head into the steel hawser with the same casual force. It's a good warning to watch out once I get into wilder territory.

The deck of the bridge is only about forty centimetres wide and maybe thirty metres long and I'm tempted to cycle across. I set off over the bridge and pretty soon discover why riding, instead of walking, is not a great idea – the bridge is lightly built and quite lively in response to having over a hundred and ten kilos of man, bike and luggage tentatively pedalled across it. The side rails lean out at a decent angle from the narrow deck and my hind brain is convinced that because the sides aren't vertical they're not actually there at all. It feels as if one slip on the bridge, which I can now feel rippling and squirming underneath me, is going to see me taking a plunge into the water below, which is heading to the sea with oily, muscular intent. I remember my resolve from before and get off to push the rig over. It's a ridiculous process because the deck isn't actually wide enough for me to walk beside the bike as I push it and I'm forced to adopt a sort of ballroom lockstep shuffle, not totally compatible with any ideas I might have of being a steely-eyed explorer.

At the other end of the bridge a steel staircase leads down to the level of the bank. Things descend, as they so often must, into sweaty farce on the way down the twenty-odd steps leading to the sheep paddock. I have to unhitch the trailer from the bike to get both down the stairs. When it's hitched and running on smooth ground, the trailer is barely noticeable, but unhitch it and try to use it as a trolley and it flops around like an amorous drunk writhing on a sofa as you try to get them to bed. Once the rig is re-assembled there's a feeling of the journey maybe finally starting properly. The comedy interlude is surely over and the serious mountain cycling can begin. Or at least it can once we're out of the sheep paddock.

There are two possible ways of getting out. One involves another gate and some unrideable steps right in front of the picture windows of the café of the Inverawe smokehouse. The other way means a half-mile saunter downriver before doubling back. I reckon that there's nothing at all to be gained by providing slapstick entertainment for the tourists enjoying their smoked trout salads. There's a lovely meandering single track through the field, strewn with sheep's dirt and perfumed with that earthy reek only sheep fields have. There's even a little ford across a river and it's very satisfying to plough straight through, confident in the bike, the tyres and the waterproof kitbag on the trailer.

Once we're clear of the field, it really does start to feel like we're under way, a feeling that's only increased as the charming single-track road under mixed oak and pines takes a sharp left turn and I find myself rapidly rattling through the gears – though I start to feel the bike being held back by the six days' worth of camping gear in the baggage train. And this is on tarmac, before we get onto the looser and less accommodating surfaces of the trail ahead. It still feels like a bit of a jaunt, though a slightly uneasy one. I realise that I won't actually feel I'm on my way until I cross my first watershed tomorrow. Today's only ever going to be a prelude.

The tarmac undulates through lovely broadleaved woods along the banks of the Awe up to the unremarkable T-junction where we'll turn into the wilds. It's here that we point our bikes away from the cafés, B&Bs and mobile reception and head off towards the interior. There's a deer gate to be negotiated and that's it. In five minutes all trace of town life is gone, with a sea loch sparkling on one side and a mountain looming on the other, an impression that lasts for about ten minutes until we find an enormous Caterpillar digger blocking the entire width of the track. The driver's nowhere to be seen and a passage past is impossible without unhitching my load for the second time in about four kilometres – there seems little doubt that this will be the *leitmotif* for the whole journey. Still, obstacles do not exist to be surrendered to, they exist to be overcome, as a good friend of mine once got in trouble for saying.

The release latches that clip the trailer to the modified rear axle of the bike are clever enough and not too hard to disengage, but when you take the first one off, the trailer inevitably loses what little stability it has – it's stuffed to bursting with food and shelter – and dives wildly to the side like it's been shot, twisting the remaining hitch into a hard-to-release position. But it eventually succumbs. I squeeze the bike past the digger first and go back for the trailer. It really isn't designed to move any other way than attached to the back of a bicycle and it does a weird, fatigued back flip as I try to get hold of it.

At that moment the driver of the digger turns up, full of Highland good manners. He's blocked my way, it's too late to move his vehicle and so he does the only thing a gentleman could do in the circumstances. He picks up the twenty-six-kilogram beast of a trailer like it was a baby and carries it around the obstruction. I'm deskbound for much of my life, and he's a young manual worker, but the difference in the size of our arms is shocking. It's quite clear it's like picking up a bag of shopping would be for me. I thank him for his effort and he nods.

Nathalie's always been keen on big machines and tries her luck getting a go at the controls of the digger. If you attempted any such thing in a town, all you'd get is an explanation of the finer points of health and safety legislation, but here, just a few miles from the tarmac, you can feel the strength of Lowland rules ebbing and the strengthening of gentler, more human Highland ways. So he regrets to inform her that they're busy right now but also promises her a shot when she's on the way back to the car tomorrow. True or not, that's a good outcome for everyone. We've all got what we want and it hasn't cost anyone anything.

One of the things I'm keen to do on this trip is to make contact with everyone I come across. The territory I'll be crossing is wild, but there are bound to be a few folk on the trails, and I'm particularly interested in anyone coming the other way on the same path as me. Just as we clear the digger obstruction, a young lady comes the other way pushing an old, green, steel-framed mountain bike. But with the digger driver in the cab and raring to get back to work I'm distracted and barely make eye contact with her, let alone say hello or get into conversation. She's not carrying much luggage and I don't think she can have been camping last night, but I feel a bit of failure for not engaging with her to find out what the trail is like ahead. Is it rideable? Is it fun? It's too late now, and she didn't really seem to be up for a chat anyway, but I resolve to get a couple of words at least from anyone else I meet on the way.

The road up the east side of Loch Etive never really gets much more than fifty metres above the sea. After the first climb, you can pretty much see the whole length of the fjord laid out to the north. The track has a multitude of climbs up to that fifty-metre limit and a surface that seems to be mainly some kind of rubble, which makes for an energy-sapping ride. There isn't that far to go – twenty-five kilometres, at most – but for some reason I find myself agitated, impatient to steam ahead.

What's happening is that my anxiety is getting the better of me. I'm a town cyclist, not some hard-core bikepacker, and we're crossing terrain that I just don't know beyond the maps and the handful of internet images I've found. In the back of my head is the very real possibility that for any one of a hundred possible reasons, from raging rivers to injury to mechanical problems, I won't make it. Despite the exceptional scenery and the total freedom of the days ahead, I can't bring myself to relax and immerse myself in the journey as I'd planned. Also, in my mind I've been thinking of this as a solo trip where the one thing I don't have to worry about is how anyone else is feeling, which will be fine for the days to come but which is stupid and selfish now Nathalie is with me.

The road continues to rise and fall but there are three distinct points along it. On the whole of the journey my waypoints are the river crossings and the watersheds where I'll cross from one river's catchment into its neighbour's. Along Loch Etive we need to cross the Noe, Liver and Kinglass and the two headlands between them before turning inland. The bridge over the Noe is barely notice-able, just a wooded dip in the track with a bit of lateral fencing, and the lush deciduous woodland is thick enough to pretty much hide the river itself. Glen Noe itself is owned by a small family trust, but the track leads on to the vast estates controlled by vari-ous members of the Fleming family, originally investment bankers in Dundee, whose members include Ian Fleming, the author of the James Bond novels. He must have passed this way himself often enough and I can't help thinking he missed a trick by giving Dr No the name Julius rather than Glen.

There's a short jink inland to pass in front of the Noe estate buildings and then the magnificent sight of the track rising directly in front of us over the sea loch, with the oak and birch forest on the lower slopes of the other side of Loch Etive behind it. Looking back to where we've just come from, there is the north side of Ben Cruachan, the mountain famously hollowed out in the sixties for a hydroelectric scheme. The main road to Oban passes right in front of the south face, but you don't get the full sense of quite how high it is from that close. From here, it's impressively tall and wild.

Up until the early years of the twentieth century, maps show nothing more than a footpath, if that, leading round the headland from Glen Noe to Glen Liver, and you can see why. The present Land Rover track has been blasted into the hillside to keep the gradient manageable, but all the same it's a bit sweaty grinding up it. Halfway to what I suppose is the curve around the headland – the point where the road just seems to stop in mid-air – there's a freshly crushed slow-worm on the track. Its upper body has been squashed and its innards are spilled quite neatly around it as it squirms in agony, no doubt run over by one of the tradesman's vans that have just rather incongruously come the other way after a day's work on a shooting lodge higher up the glen. It may just be a lizard and close to death, but its suffering is intolerable to me and I open my folding knife and kill it the quickest way I can think of, cutting its head clean off. The body keeps on writhing gently but I still think it was the compassionate thing to do.

It's upsetting to feel obliged to kill such a beautiful animal, only the second slow-worm I have ever seen in this country. I'm always bowled over by the incredible metallic bronze sheen of their skin, more like something you'd see on a beetle's carapace than on a reptile, deep and iridescent, and I'm lost in these thoughts as I crest the headland and run down into Glen Liver, across the wooden bridge and round the small bay. It's like something out of a garden centre, fringed with irises and thick, low bushes.

We climb up to the next headland between the Liver and the Kinglass and we are rewarded with the most glorious vista up towards the head of Loch Etive. Looking down, there is low-lying grassland fringed with scrubby oak trees next to sandy bays, with the looming mass of Ben Starav in the background. The mouth of the Kinglass is in front of us, a deep, dark channel. In the distance is a magnificent conical mountain with another behind. It takes me a moment with the OS map to figure out that what I'm looking at is probably Stob Dubh, the southern summit of Buachaille Etive Beag, which overlooks the pass of Glencoe. Every tourist that has ever come to the Highlands has seen this mountain, but from the other side, where the road runs right in front of it. We've come far enough to start getting alternative perspectives on familiar things, and I hope there will be a lot more of them to come.

Freewheeling down to the wooden bridge over the river is a delight. It's just the right gradient and surface to pick up some speed, with the added pleasure of knowing that this is the first milestone on the journey. This is where we'll turn our backs on the sea and head inland, cutting across a country I know well but on paths that will be new to me. This is also where the vertical profile of the route starts its erratic progress to the summit of the Gaick Pass five hundred metres above us and a hundred and thirty kilometres away.

Incongruously with the wild setting, there's a kind of rustic billboard before the bridge proclaiming *Wild game management* and requesting that dogs should stay on the lead. If the game really was wild, it maybe wouldn't have much to fear from most domestic dogs. The bulk of the game round here isn't that much wilder than the sheep, which is maybe the real concern. Only the rabbits and the roe deer are properly wild, and they're treated more like vermin.

It's funny, but I've always felt a connection to certain rivers. To the Dee, maybe because it's my home one, and to the Findhorn, whose slightly absurd name I have liked since I was a child. That connection is partly why I was pleased to choose its mouth as the end-destination of this trip. The Findhorn is a magnificent, properly Highland river in its upper stretches that runs out into a big, flat, muddy bay like some soft southerner. I've slept beside the Findhorn so far up into its catchment that I could step over it in the morning. I'm delighted to find that the Kinglass is equally enchanting. Looking down from the bridge, it has a calm poise about it. It's maybe six feet deep and the colour of weak tea, totally transparent and fit for huge, sleek salmon to make their way up in the wee small hours. It would be very tempting to cast a trout fly in here if I had a rod in my kit.

Although it's quite deserted now, apart from the gamekeeper's house at Ardmaddy a few hundred metres away, Inverkinglass played its part in two thriving international industries during the eighteenth century. The woods, which grew thick on the north side of the river, were first sold in 1721 to an Irish partnership headed by a Dubliner who needed oak bark for his leather-tanning business. It branched out quickly to encompass charcoal-fuelled iron smelting before collapsing in the depression of 1737. Then a Lancashire firm revived and expanded iron smelting here, in around 1753. The first Statistical Account from the turn of the eighteenth century was possibly the first time anyone tried to get a detailed picture of the country's society – who lived where and what they had and what they did – through a series of numerical essays on the habits of the people of each parish written by its minister. The account for the parish we're in – Ardchattan and Muckairn – notes with some sadness that the low ground in the area ceased to be cultivated, but was rented out instead for grazing the foundry's work horses. The land 'lies waste and uncultivated; and occasions the importation of a considerable amount of meal into that district'. Unfortunately, this seems to pretty much cover the situation today. The land is given over to the leisure pursuits of the wealthy, with a certain tolerance for the outdoor eccentricities of city dwellers like me.

After Culloden and the military occupation that followed, there was a general realisation by the state that data was needed to describe and understand the country. The Statistical Account prefigured the census we know, and the Roy military survey was undoubtedly the precursor of the Ordnance Survey. Teams of British army surveyors working between 1747 and 1755 produced the first accurate maps of the Highlands, made with watercolour and ink. I have five OS maps, direct descendants of those ones, bundled in an elastic band in the trailer, and a sixth in a waterproof case, as my daily guides through the hills.

The second iron forge is marked on the Roy map of Glen Kinglass, along with the reason for its location: oak forests for charcoal. Our world runs on oil and gas, but two hundred and fifty years ago people looked at a Highland oak wood and saw energy for industry where we would see a beautiful landscape. At the time, charcoal was the only fuel known to be suitable for smelting, so the industry had to be near forests to be economical. Once the trees were gone, the sheep moved in. Now deer have replaced the sheep and the trees are still struggling, though there's good cover here at the mouth of the river. The scene around us is as green and pleasant as any part of the country, utterly tranquil and uninhabited, but it was a hive of industry just a few hundred years ago. Hard to believe though it is, we're in a post-industrial landscape.

* * *

It's only a short distance up the glen to the planned stop for the night – a bothy three kilometres away. The track up is loose but easy to ride, closely hemmed in by the trees at the start but opening out with a great view up the glen in the evening sunshine. Bothies come in all shapes and sizes and all states of repair, and what little I've found online gives only a vague picture of the state of the building. When we reach the location, it is not that easy to spot as it's set back some way from the track and nestled in among some mature broadleaved woods that run down from the steep crag above. The crag is cut in two by the gorge of the Allt Narrachan in a way that reminds me of Chinese silk painting, with the strong diagonal of the stream flicking from side to side before leaping off into a waterfall with trees perched either side on crazy ledges, the whole thing draped in half-formed or half-dispersed clouds. It is utterly bewitching.

There's a long-forgotten field of rough, tussocky grass between the track and the bothy itself, and the kidney-swilling lurch across it, with the suspension squeaking and groaning in the perfectly still Highland evening, is a lovely end to the first day's cycling. The thing with bothies is that you never quite know what you're going to find. It may be that the bothy burnt down the day before or got trashed, but what you usually find is a rough shelter in perfect order, and sometimes there will be a couple of candles, some packet food or even a can of beer.

The outside aspect of the building is in perfect keeping with the surroundings. It's a traditional cruck-framed cottage, likely from the era of the iron foundry. The cruck-frame design allowed people with timber but no cement to build cottages where the roof beams sat straight on the ground, and the stone walls were built to fill the gaps in the timber structure rather than to bear any weight. They were usually faced with clay, but that washed away years ago on this bothy. You can see where boulders the size of steamer trunks have been set down to make the outline of the four walls and the rest built up with rucksack-sized stones from the riverbed. As a result, the corners are projected and rounded, and the walls seem to slope back as they rise. The lack of pointing or rendering makes the whole construction look like something talented children have put together on a dry riverbed, and it has an organic feel to it. The modern corrugated iron roof comes right down to the level of the door, which has no lintel. As I move to open the latch, a mouse, disturbed in the long grass, shoots into the space between two boulders in the wall. Anyone squeamish about sharing with mice or spiders might be best advised to avoid bothies altogether, but they'd be missing out on one of the great pleasures of the Highlands.

Because bothies are open to any traveller to use, you never know who's in residence. It's polite to knock, so I do and wait for a reply that doesn't come. It feels like we are completely alone here, apart from the mice. I duck under the projecting edge of the roof and step in and down onto the floor, which is what the French would call *terre battue* if it was beaten a bit more. It's actually fine, dry earth. My first instinct on entering a bothy is to have a good sniff. This place smells clean and dry. It's dim but there are a couple of neatly fitted windows made from corrugated PVC sheet. The interior décor is sparse but functional – three benches made from a pair of logs and a plank each, a couple of coffee tables of the same design, a rustic fireplace and a couple of branches that have been taken inside to dry. The inside surface of the walls has been neatly pointed with cement and the whole place is wind- and watertight. Some bothies have wooden floors, interior walls even, and furniture. This is the real thing, just a dry shelter open to any passing traveller.

The first thing to do is to figure out where we're sleeping and lay out the sleeping mats and bags. I can't sleep at all with my feet above my head by so much as a centimetre, so gradient is the main factor for me, though avoiding lumps and bumps in the floor is also important. The floor has been dished by years of feet wearing down the middle, so the best place seems to be under the skylight with our heads next to the fireplace. It's warm enough that I'll not bother trying to get a blaze going, but it is tempting, just for the atmosphere and the emotional centre point that a lit hearth gives, a focus that's lacking when you're somewhere so unfamiliar and utterly spartan.

We're both out of our stable orbits and I've got that distinct feeling of liberation and anxiety about not knowing quite what to do when I arrive somewhere wild. The constant certainty with cycling is that whatever else you do, you're going to have to eat, and eat plenty. Wild campers can be divided into two types depending on how they heat their food. There's the spirit stove mob and the gas canister gang. I'm firmly in the spirit stove camp because I appreciate the rugged simplicity of the classic Swedish army design. It barely has any moving parts and although it's designed to run on methylated spirit, it can burn pretty much any flammable liquid, though petrol might get quite exciting. The whole thing nests up inside itself like a domestic Russian doll of diminutive teapot, saucepans, burner, stand, pan handle and frying pan, and it barely makes any noise in your bag as you move. It just seems to be the paradigm of good design – robust, simple, repair-able and adaptable, if not the most powerful. It's the bicycle of the stove world.

My rations on this trip are designed to keep the amount of water I'm transporting to a minimum, using dried pasta as the basis of my dinner each night with a small tub of sauce to liven it up, though I'm keeping a freeze-dried wild mushroom risotto as a treat for dinner on the third night when, if all goes well, I should be at the halfway stage. Tonight, I'm cooking my pasta in the sweet water from the Allt Narrachan that runs right behind the bothy, along with a good dose of salt to make up for the after-noon's sweat. I never seem to learn and yet again take the hairs off the backs of my fingers as I light the alcohol in the burner and the clear, almost invisible flame licks quickly over my hand.

With the inverted frying pan as a cover and a gentle breeze fanning the flame, the water boils quicker than expected, the lid chiming musically against the pan rim as the steam escapes. Each day's pasta ration of one hundred and fifty grams of fusilli is in its own knotted plastic bag to stop me getting greedy and running out. Waiting for it to cook is very satisfying, sat as I am on a tumbledown wall thickly upholstered with moss in the middle of nowhere, knowing that a hot meal will be ready in quarter of an hour.

Nathalie's approach to food, and indeed most things, is joyously different to mine. Arrayed on the wall beside her are, in no particular order, three cold boiled Désirée potatoes in their skins, a whole Camembert cheese, oatcakes, Brussels pâté, gherkins and pickled onions, clementines and a tub of 'all-purpose savoury seasoning'. There's more than a hint of jazz improvisation about it and I'd be tempted to ask for a swap if I didn't know the low esteem in which she holds my pasta addiction.

Some bikepackers worship at the altar of weight reduction, drilling holes in their sporks and cutting the handles off their toothbrushes. They sleep under simple flysheets suspended from trees and rocks. I swear by proper cutlery and decent red wine, though I make a nod in the direction of weight reduction by decanting the wine into a plastic lemonade bottle, the top carefully sealed with cling film. I've marked up the bottle with gradated masking tape strips in an effort to stop myself accidentally over-consuming on any given evening. There is, it has to be said, something deeply right and proper about drinking at wild campsites after the effort to reach them, and my self-discipline is not good.

Draining the cooking water from the pasta onto the turf immediately feels wrong, like an insult to the land. I don't suppose it will actually kill the grass, but you never know and I won't do it again. Stirring the sauce into the hot macaroni releases an out-of-place domestic smell into the still air and all I need now is to pour us some of the wine and we'll be set. The first mouthful of hot food and sip of wine purge all the anxiety from my body and mind. I hadn't realised how intense I'd been feeling about the bike, finding the way, the bothy and the responsibility of leading Nathalie on tracks I didn't know myself, but having food and drink in my stomach just seems to give me permission to see those fears, acknowledge them and let them go.

The evening is mild and windless and the clouds low, and just one thing is missing from this Highland tableau. Although there was a very persistent gleg (a sturdy, grey, biting fly with the cruelly mechanical look of a Messerschmitt fighter plane) that had to be stalked and killed as it got ready to slice into the back of my leg, there's not a midge to be seen, heard or felt in what ought to be the epicentre of their kingdom. Part of the reason that the west coast is quite so deserted, despite its obvious attractions, is the fact that it's only very occasionally pleasant or easy to be outdoors. Only rarely do you get a moment where it's not cold, wet, windy or midge-infested. The first two weeks of May are prized by holiday home owners as the only time when it's likely you might get a barbecue without getting eaten yourself. The worst time is undoubtedly when the midges come out in warm midsummer rain and you find yourself assailed by innumerable barely visible micro-vampires, each one keen to make its way inside your rainwear for a feast. Zip your jacket up and you swelter like the boil-in-the-bag meal for one million that you are; let the air in and the little horrors come in with it. There are moments when they're so dense that you think they're going to clog your nostrils. The best repellents only stop them biting rather than discouraging them from massing in your ears, your nose and round your hairline. The only real defence is to use a head net and mesh gloves. Given I'll be outdoors for the best part of a week, I'm carrying both for this trip, but they get in the way of wilderness drinking and I'm glad not to have to use them now.

Once the dishes are washed in the burn and stowed for breakfast, it seems only right and natural to take a short, romantic stroll to get a sense of the scenery and to luxuriate in the simple isolation, just twenty kilometres from a railway and a trunk road. I get changed into a pair of light trousers and a long-sleeved top that I've packed for the inevitable midge assault and we set out up the glen. It is simply beautiful. Not in the slap-in-the-face picture postcard way that Glencoe is, but there's a verdant intimacy about the flat ground either side of the river, with the rugged foothills of Ben Starav to the north and the gentler hills to the south. The floor of the glen is carpeted in lush, green grass that comes up to our knees and in which each wave of the breeze is visible as it rolls down the glen and into the scrubby oaks and alders, their leaves flashing their silvery undersides in ripples. So many people have an idea of the Highlands as being a heather monoculture but this is a million miles from that, surely the remnants of the forest whose timber once fuelled the iron foundry.

There's an effortless joy in just standing still and letting the landscape – weird and familiar at the same time – seep into us. Wandering slowly through the tussock grass, we come across the clear impression of a deer that's been resting there, quite possibly until just a few minutes ago, out of sight and out of the wind. We could curl up together in the green saucer and see nothing but the clouds ambling across a blue sky now tinged with pink as the sun goes down.

With all the normal domestic cues of clocks and television left behind, the question of when to turn in for the night is a biological one. You lie down to sleep when you're tired and it's dark enough.

And you definitely turn in if the midges come out, which they do *en masse* right on the stroke of nine. That's a compromise I can live with and if the next few days see the same late-evening kick-off for the midge festival, I'll be quite content. It may only have been a few hours' ride to get here, but I'm not spectacularly fit right now and I can feel the fatigue not so much in my legs as in my haunches, my back, my loins and my head – the bits of me that have been working the hardest today.

I'm a total sucker for comfort in bed, even in the wilds. I've never found sleeping bags to be quite warm enough in our climate and I've taken to carrying a pair of fleece pyjama trousers to sleep in, along with my usual array of warm tops. It's just as well I've got these as the zip on my sleeping bag choses this exact moment – the first night of the trip – to come away in my hand. I've got my first bit of kit failure of the trip. There are bound to be others and I'm carrying a tool kit, cable ties and a bit of tent repair tape in anticipation, but there's nothing to be done here other than tucking the loose flap of the sleeping bag under my body and trying to get comfortable.

Although there's no lack of physical comfort and I've got Nathalie snoozing right beside me, I just can't get to sleep. I've pored over maps and read books and even watched videos online but I still can't stop my mind racing back and forwards over the profile of the ride and lingering over the sketchy bits where there's a prospect of things going wrong – an impassable river, an unrideable bog or a navigational error in some wilderness. The sound of the burn just a few metres away is a great lullaby but sleep just will not come.

Eventually the noise of running water is joined by the rhythmic rattle of rain on the bothy's black tin roof. The rain's a worry. Not from the point of view of getting wet – I'm all kitted up for that – but just because I've at least a couple of unbridged rivers to cross tomorrow, so this new noise stokes a fresh dread: that I'll head off on my own in the morning, only to have to turn back at the first proper obstacle. Fording rivers on my own is certainly one of the most dangerous parts of the trip and if there's any prospect of me being swept away or breaking my ankle on unseen greasy boulders then I've promised myself I'll wait for the water to go down and turn back if my food runs out while I'm waiting. Rivers round here can rise very quickly indeed and they're not exactly empty right now.

The rain and my mind skimming over a landscape I know in theory but not in practice combine to make for a fitful sort of fever dream, and when I regain some sort of sanity around six, I can't really tell whether I've slept or not.

Two

Breadalbane

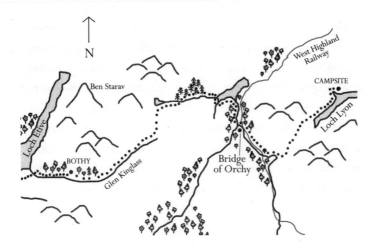

It is always earlier in the morning than I think when there are no curtains. I doze for a bit before the pressure in my bladder lifts me out of my sleeping bag. Without a bed or a seat there's a bit of fumbling and grunting just getting my shoes on. Nothing is simple, and trying not to put anything down on the earth floor adds another complication, but after a few minutes I'm up and unlatching the door to step out into Glen Kinglass.

It would be odd enough getting up at home and going straight out of my own front door, but the sense of dislocation in stepping under the low lintel and out into the West Highlands is dizzying. The landscape's eyes are hidden but we are looking at each other anyway, the lush glen like a theatre stage set after the play's fin-ished and both players and audience have gone home. The simple act of stepping through a door has put me through the looking glass and I'm filled with a gentle wonder at being alone with the grass, the trees and the rocks. The sense of isolation and containment is almost perfect, with the low clouds forming a canopy over the glen's steep sides. The pleasure is doubled by knowing that Nathalie, slumbering safe and dry in the rugged bothy, still has this experience to come.

I've felt vaguely grubby since about twenty minutes after we set out, and a warm afternoon's cycling on dusty tracks followed by a night in an unzipped sleeping bag on an earth floor has done nothing to make me feel any cleaner. The burn tumbling down the hill to the pool behind the bothy has what I need. There's a rock just right to kneel on and cold, sweet water that I cup in both hands and dip my face in, washing away the grimy crust. The trees form a vaulted roof over the river and it's like washing in some fantastic spa sanctuary – half ceremony, half everyday ablution.

There's no way of avoiding the everyday, not even here. Cycling in rough country consumes thousands of calories and I'm pretty sure that I'm going to spend a good part of the trip either being hungry or eating. I've always found having hot food first thing to be comforting in the hills, and I've planned to have that great British camping classic each morning – baked beans and sausages. One thing I've learned is that camping food in general, and this dish in particular, is always made to cater to the tastes of three-year-old children. It's far too sweet and I've come equipped to add salt, flavour and acidity to the packets each morning. The salt comes in a handy three-way cruet shaker with room for another powder besides that and pepper. I've chosen one of my favourite spices – smoked paprika – to add a bit of depth. Besides that, I've got brown sauce, packed with tamarind and vinegar.

The mere fact of being here in this place early on a still morning is psychoactive, but in a calming, meditative way. If I'm going to get myself organised and under way, I'll need something more stimulating. My taste in the outdoors is always to have alcohol in the evening and caffeine in the morning. The caffeine is the more vital of the two, and I don't think I've missed many days of my *café au lait* habit since a German friend at university showed me how to make it properly thirty years ago. Espresso and hot milk are out of the question here, but the packet cappuccinos you can buy now aren't bad – though they need a couple of spoons of decent freeze-dried coffee to be satisfying. My coppery alloy mug is absolutely rubbish for hot drinks as the handle heats up almost instantly, but I've always been oddly loyal to inanimate objects and it is my camping cup so I wrap a cycling mitt round the scalding metal and pretend that's entirely normal while the boil-in-the-bag beans heat up on the stove. With added salt, paprika and a good squirt of the sauce, they're not too bad. Welcome in fact, and gone in a couple of minutes.

I haven't shirked on weight for this trip because comfort is far more important to me than speed, but all the same there's no room for waste and pretty much everything has to have at least two functions. My sleeping mat is also a seat when folded up. The flat underside of the trailer becomes a table when turned upside down. The cable and padlock become a weapon, in fantasy if not in reality, should any farm dogs take too close an interest in me – something that has happened before. The water my breakfast heats up in has to double as my washing water. There's no delicate way of saying it, but six days' cycling on rough ground is punishing on your backside. It's vital to keep your undercarriage clean and healthy, so after a trip into the woods behind the bothy, with an ancient dinner knife as a stand-in lightweight trowel, it's time for a quick wash with the still-warm cooking water, lathered up with a squirt of liquid soap.

My rule for figuring out how long it takes to get going in the morning is to work out how long it will take me to do it on my own, then double that, and raise it to the power of the number of people in the group. In this case that means four times my estimate of forty-five minutes. I'm sure the army has ways to get that number down involving shouting and training, but I'm not all that interested in either. Hopeful, expectant pottering and fiddling with kit is a great way to start any day and that's just what I do while Nathalie gets herself ready to face the ride back to the car, leaving me to head on up the Kinglass and over into Glen Orchy.

Everything is stowed in the trailer with the weight as low and as far back as possible for stability, and so that the single wheel of the trailer bears the brunt of the load. The rear wheel of the bike will have enough to deal with, given that I'll be sitting on top of it for the next few days. Everything that I might need to get a hand on quickly is in my rucksack: camera, binoculars, maps and water bottle. One thing I will never be far away from – in fact one thing that I'll often be up to my knees in – is water, so the water bottle is half empty to keep the weight down. The weight of water shouldn't really come as a surprise at my age, but it always does.

Eventually, at about ten, both of us have finished faffing with bungee cords, nylon straps and buckles. We take the bothy rules to heart and the place has to be spotless and shipshape or as close as an earth-floored hut can get to that state before we leave. There can be no litter, no disorder. To leave the place any other way is an insult to yourself, the owner and the next user. This bothy belongs to a Fleming, and I wonder if he's ever spent the night here. I hope he has.

Once we're convinced there's no visible trace of our night under the tin roof, we roll our bikes down to the estate road. I'll turn left and take off on my own into the wilds and Nathalie will turn right and head back the way we came in. I tell her to be careful, but it's hard to keep my mind from wandering to the high ground that lies ahead. I can feel the determined, selfish arsehole part of me – the bit I actually need to get myself to Findhorn – coming out of the woodwork. It's probably best for both of us to get going, so I send Nathalie on her way with a kiss and watch her ride off down the glen towards the sea, the car and home. We're due to meet in two days' time, but the roads we'll take to get to our rendezvous are quite different. I'd best skedaddle myself if I'm going to make it. With a last look at the departing figure, I turn my mind and my body to the journey in front of me.

* * *

The Land Rover track makes for good going and there's no navigation needed until I get to Kinglass shooting lodge; it's just a question of turning the pedals over and watching the world put itself gently behind me. In all, there's about two hundred metres' climb from the bothy to the watershed, which is nothing much in cycling terms, but still the equivalent of climbing from the base of Arthur's Seat to the top, not something many people would volunteer to do on a bicycle dragging camping kit and a week's rations.

As I set off, the track is closely fringed with hazel and alder but it opens out. Pretty soon the lodge comes into view along with a couple of peculiar waterfalls behind it, as if the river is running down the steps of a half-buried ziggurat. I'd guess that the whole glen is composed of successive lava flows but it looks like the power of the river has scoured away the mountains' surface to reveal the contour lines on the Ordnance Survey map.

When I get close enough to the lodge to see it properly, it is oddly utilitarian, clearly the result of a process of accretion rather than any plan. There's what seems to be the main house, built in stone, which faces the higher north side of the glen rather than the view down the river back to the sea. Tacked onto this are a couple of extensions that must double the size of the building, and behind are what seem to be workers' cottages, another house and a tiny block with two doors that must surely have been a toilet block. It's hard not to project a hierarchy of occupation onto the premises, with the laird in the big house, his guests in the outbuilding, the head keeper in the small house and the keepers in the cottages, maybe without indoor sanitation. The place just reeks of rank and Victorian social order; and with the whitewash, the recently mowed lawns and surrounding deer fence, it does have the air of a military compound as much as a sporting lodge. Behind the lodge is a small pine wood, the trees growing tall and straight, an obvious contrast with the twisted deciduous trees lower down the glen. Nothing crooked or shabby seems to be allowed here.

Past the lodge, the track over the head of the glen obviously hasn't seen much vehicle traffic recently. I'm on what was the main road into Glen Kinglass on the 1906 Ordnance Survey map, before the track over the headland between Glen Noe and Glen Liver was blasted in. That's so long ago that there is also a school marked nearby on the same map, but there are no children here now and I think I might be the only adult.

The surface is turf and half-sunk boulders and the bike's suspension starts to whistle and chirp as I drop down into the lowest gear, the rolling resistance and gradient picking up at the same time. The obstacles start to show themselves, first in the shape of the Eas a' Bhinnein, racing down its rocky channel. There's a bridge, but it's like something out of an assault course. It's made from the trunk of a pine that's been split in half and laid down, with steeply sloping hawser and wire mesh sides. I'd guess that real mountain bikers, as opposed to mountain cyclists like me, would regard this as a challenge and hammer across it, but the last thing I need is to run off it and gouge a hole in myself with the crude wire rigging. And in any case, there's no one here to be impressed by any bike handling skills I might or might not have. The safest option is to unhitch the trailer and pull it across first, and carefully too, given that the surface of the split trunk is greasy with decay and spray from the burn hurtling underneath.

After the bridge, the track narrows to a footpath and I get into a delightful rhythmic, almost hypnotic state, just turning the cranks and looking four or five metres ahead to pick out a line with the flattest profile and the best traction. The whole hillside is draining across the path, which is mostly under an inch or two of water. After a while I come to a place that I recognise from Phil McKane's book: the McMoab slabs. Moab is a centre for sports mountain bikers in Utah renowned for trails running over bare desert sandstone. But here, basalt rocks, ankle-deep in running water, make for a wry reflection of that parched place, though the smile is wiped from my face by a massive slide as my rear tyre gives up on a section of submerged polished rock covered in slime, and the whole rig takes a wild lurch to the right. I catch it in time and put a foot down, but the Vibram soles of my shoes don't get much more grip than the tyres. The surface is more like ice than desert rock, and I ride off gingerly onto the more conventional track that leads on up to the head of the glen, where I'll finally get to see the watershed.

The accounts of this trail are all rather cryptic and the OS map isn't entirely clear on what happens when it comes to crossing the Kinglass and heading up to the col. There seem to be two bridges close together, but one is reputed to be in a state of disrepair and I'm hoping it's very obvious which one is the more trustworthy.

As I keep going up, the country keeps opening out and getting bleaker, with boggy moorland replacing the rough grassland lower down. The track widens out again and there are traces of vehicles, but they must have come from somewhere else on the estate. A fork to the right almost doubles back down the glen, but I'm pretty sure it leads to the bridge that's my best option to cross the Kinglass, so I roll down that way, hoping not to have to pedal the whole way back up again. I'm not disappointed – there's a bridge and it is a stout affair built of timber beams on steel girders spanning a rocky defile with the river crashing along four or five metres below. It hasn't got any kind of guard rails and even though it's quite wide enough for a Jeep to get over, I feel a bit uneasy. Given that I've just picked my way with a precision of a centimetre or two over a treacherous rocky track, the chances of me making a steering error of a metre and a half on a dry, flat timber bridge are minimal, but that is not the way my brain sees things. If I ride my bike off this bridge into the river, I will undoubtedly die. The bit of my brain that deals with immediate risks to life doesn't seem to be too interested in how likely they are, just how close they are. Luckily, there are other bits of my brain I can call on to tell that part not to worry while I carry out the entirely banal operation of cycling a short distance across a flat surface. But there's still a voice in the background saying loud and clear, 'You'll die if you get this wrong.'

I roll off the bridge and straight into a clump of heather. Surely there's been some mistake. I cast an eye around for the track. Nothing. Not a road, not a track, not a path, not a tyre track, not a footprint. Absolutely nothing. It's a temporary difficulty, surely? I raise my eyes and scan the terrain for the inevitable trace of the track a little farther off. There is heather, there is sphagnum moss, there are rocks peeping out of the peat on the slopes. There is bog myrtle, that finely perfumed sign of intractable ground, and there is tussock grass – lots of it – but there is no track.

I unsling my pack and get the binoculars out, convinced that the path must be either hiding or fleeing up the hill somewhere, but making a circuit of the horizon to try to spot where it cuts the line of the hill just leaves me disoriented. I squint at the map, which swims and ripples a bit in front of me. Surely it can't be that complex? The bridge was a good one so that was right. The path on the map crosses the watershed so if I just keep going I'll find it, won't I? I stow the binoculars and cast a quick eye over the ground in front of me. It is not promising, a mixture of sucking bog and hummocks the size of armchairs. I push the bike forward into the moorland, feeling the tension in my shoulders and the bunching of my thigh muscles as I test what kind of effort is going to be needed to make progress over this uncooperative vegetation. The idea starts to form that I want to be in Bridge of Orchy for lunchtime and that this sopping morass is an unreasonable obstacle to that goal. I put my head down and allow the part of my brain which engages in sheer bloody-mindedness to take over. I call it the *corpus intransigens* and it is well-developed in most cyclists.

People never seem to look at moorland properly. They always think it's a khaki-coloured, monotonous carpet of heather or grass, but it isn't at all. The closer you look, the wilder it is, and I do look closely as I'm doubled over the bars of the bike so that I can inch it over the unsuitable terrain, my eyes close to the ground. The colours and shapes of the various mosses and lichens are staggering, ranging from acid green to pillar box red and imperial purple. That's khaki at a distance but up close it's verging on psychedelic. The beauty of it is a welcome distraction, but I can feel the sweat starting to rise on my back despite the cool upland air, and my mind turns to what I might get for lunch as I drive the bike and trailer forward.

After a certain time, whose limits I would not know, I come to a halt and look up. Nothing much has changed, I'm on my own in a bog with hills on two sides and a low ridge up ahead, surrounded by exposed rock, tussock grass and tiny wee lochans filled with water the colour of eighty shilling. I'm normally a very confident – occasionally over-confident – navigator, but right now I'm really not at all sure that this is the right way. The sweat starts to break on my hands, not out of effort, but out of fear that I've just ploughed God-knows-how-far off track on my first morning riding solo over country I've been studying on paper for a year. The reality is that I've nothing to fear physically, given that I'm equipped to sit right down and spend the next five days here quite comfortably in any weather. But the thought of maybe having got lost quite so soon is a damaging one for my idea of myself as someone who's comfortable in wild country. I look around in front of me – for some reason I'm forming the opinion that looking behind me is admitting defeat – and am astounded to see a signpost.

This one is peculiar in that it bears no sign at all. I am in the middle of a bog with a bicycle and a signpost with no sign. My head begins to spin with mad notions of how I've surely not been paying attention and strayed up the wrong glen. My heart rate is rising and I have to get an actual grip on myself, first making sure that I control my breathing and then sitting down for a drink of water and a serious look at the map and compass.

Orienting the map to the landscape makes matters a lot clearer. I take bearings on the surrounding summits, and the patch of planted woodland I can see, and make an estimate of the distances to the various features. I am, in fact, on the right track and only a couple of kilometres from the watershed, at most. By not keeping an eye on the map when I didn't *think* I was lost, I've got myself into a situation where I was completely disorientated for a couple of seconds. This isn't behaviour that is compatible with me getting safely to the other side of the country and I make a promise to myself not to be quite so casual about navigation in future. How can I possibly be energetic enough to get all of this kit from one coast to another but too lazy to pull the map out of the side-pocket of my rucksack every thirty minutes?

Having settled myself and reinstated the calm, managerial bit of me at the helm, I have a new determination to follow the compass bearing that I've reckoned to cross the path marked more clearly on the map than it seems to be on the landscape. It's not too long before I come across the twin ruts of what once might have been a quad bike track but which is now a stripe of lush grass through the heather. It's rideable in places, but so strewn with boulders and sinkholes that I wind up pushing for a kilometre or so, in an echo of the verdict of the English traveller John Taylor in the early 1600s on our roads: 'So uneven, stony and full of bogges, quag-mires, that a dogge with three legs will outrun a horse with foure.' It might be territory for a three-legged dog, and the repeated col-lisions between the left-side pedal and my right shin have me won-dering if such an animal might actually be better suited than me to pushing a bike through this mess.

My mind is finally put at rest when I come to the Allt Coire Beith and I can see the hills on the other side of Glen Orchy in the distance. The Allt Coire Beith is more of a small river than a burn, and the jumble of rocks it's tumbling over means this is the first time of many where I'll need to ford. I take off my waterproof trainers and get my slip-on beach shoes out of the trailer. These may not be classic wilderness kit, but they seem like a good idea to me. The thing with fording rivers on a multi-day trip is that even if you take your socks off, your shoes get soaking wet and they stay

ay, with predictable effects on comfort and morale. My plan
this trip is to take off my socks and shoes and put on a cheap
pair of beach shoes with Velcro fasteners whenever I have to get
my feet wet. I know I have to ford a couple of times this morning
and maybe fifteen more this afternoon, and this is a first test of
my tactics.

There's always something shockingly cold about the water in
Highland rivers and this stuff is no exception. But there's real
refreshing pleasure in feeling it fill the shoes as I stride out to mid-
calf depth, and the soles are perfectly good on the rocky river bed. I
am going to spend a lot of time tying shoelaces if I keep this up, but
it's a treat to put dry socks and shoes back on, a taste of the civilised
life now a couple of days behind and five days in front of me.

The track now drifts back into the realm of the reasonable,
straight and distinct ahead of me across the rock-dotted grassland up to the horizon that I'm hoping is the watershed. It's easy
enough to make progress in first gear and just as I top out, the
sweep of the next glen shows itself. Stopping to admire the view
and get my bearings, I spot a young falcon dozing on top of a large,
erratic boulder to the side of the path. The rock is taller than I am
and we're about level when the bird spots me and starts off down
the glen. A merlin, I think, given where we are, its size and the
elastic agility of its flight. They're not big enough to bother grouse
so they sometimes get left alone when other larger birds of prey
are made less welcome.

* * *

Once over the ridge it's easy to pick up quite a bit of speed on the
straight, shallow slope of the grass-covered track, and the sensation of the bike and trailer being at ease and moving freely over
the rough ground is palpable. It's not difficult to see why the guide

books suggest riding from Glen Orchy to Taynuilt when this route is done for sport. It must be much easier to climb up this way and bounce down over the bog and rubble to the Kinglass than to sweat it the other way, not to mention simpler to navigate, but I'm not here for sport so much as to let the land talk to me.

Loch Dochard makes a natural place to stop and have a look around at the new glen. I'm almost overwhelmed by the view up into the Black Mount, only made more dramatic by the lead-coloured cap of cloud hiding the peaks but emphasising the depth and scale of the corries. Remarkably, the glen and hills are carpeted in grass from wall to wall, with a single solitary wind-slanted tree visible on the far shore of the loch – a testament to the thoroughness of the iron smelters' logging and the appetites of the sheep and deer that came after them. Almost as if to add a bit of foreground interest to the scene, a flock of thirteen Canada geese is bobbing off the near-shore with apparent nonchalance at my presence. I guess no one shoots them here, or they know they're not in season.

Although it's comforting to know that I'm where I want to be and not off on some random tangent into the hills, there are still a couple of fords to be crossed, and my mind isn't quite at ease yet. It took a real effort of self-control to loosen my tunnel vision from the road ahead. I made myself stop and look around me at the grandeur of the mountain scenery, but there's a choice to be made now. It's between a bridge over the Abhainn Shira and a fording of one of its tributaries, or a fording of two tributaries and the Shira itself. It sounds obvious. Why refuse a bridge over the main river? But I've seen photos of riders using stepping stones instead, which they wouldn't do without reason.

Once down at the bridge it looks pretty straightforward. It's a sturdy, wire-stayed timber affair with proper guard rails and wide enough to ride across, though I don't bother as it has steps down at the far end, which I just clatter the whole rig down. It soon becomes clear why people avoid coming this way: I advance into slick and slippery peat for the first time, my hybrid rear tyre spinning up uselessly as I pedal like something out of a cartoon. I'm not really mentally equipped for turning back at this point, so I push on towards a plantation, where the track is marked as following a firebreak to the ford.

The passage through the wood is duly absurd, as if someone has been using the soft peat to try out their trench-building skills, and my feet sink into the cloying plowter with every step, causing me to break into a sweat, which doesn't go unremarked by that ubiquitous inhabitant of west coast woodland: the blackfly. They don't bite or sting at all; they just hang around looking to lap up your sweat and they are incredibly irritating in a dozy, passive way that the more focused midges, and even glegs, aren't. I am delighted when I eventually get to the river for a drink and a sluice of cold water over my head.

I spot a hiker about a hundred metres away who's the first person I've seen since I waved Nathalie off. I'm still rattled after getting in a sweaty fankle crossing the Kinglass, and I wave to him just to make sure he can see me and that I still exist properly. He gives me a casual wave, no doubt baffled as to why I'm hailing him, but his greeting is very welcome.

Having crossed the river in my now trusty beach shoes, the trail once again degenerates into farce. It's not peat hag this time but proper marshland with thick reeds and hidden rivulets running through it. This is absolutely no place for a bicycle but both the map and the compass are adamant that this is the way I need to keep going to pick up the estate track, and there are no other easier options in evidence. Persistence pays off when the trail transforms into a very welcome Land Rover track, and I'm just getting up a bit of speed when I come up against the sort of sign for which all bicyclists have a secret soft spot. It's a gem, in two colours and capital letters:

CYCLISTS
DOGS, CHILDREN
AND LIVESTOCK
AHEAD DISMOUNT HERE, THANKYOU.

Quite what should I make of that? Given the way that the sign points, it only seems to apply to those heading, like me, uphill. I can't be going much above walking pace, and in any case I've never ridden into a dog, child or sheep in my life. It makes me wonder what kind of terrible accident could have occurred to make anyone have this sign erected. Did someone really manage to ride out of the peat hag fast enough to crash into a sheep?

Whatever did prompt the sign, it's fairly typical of the attitude of some landowners who have never quite got their heads around the rights granted by the Land Reform Act of 2003, which lets us walk, cycle or paddle on any open land or water in our country that we like, provided that we do so reasonably. It's a classic British compromise, in fact: do what you like as long as you don't bother anyone who's not too easily bothered. There's no question of me dismounting here or anywhere else I'm not physically forced to. I'll be ambling along for the whole trip and keeping a close eye out for my canine, human and ovine fellows. And anyway, who cares more about their dog than their child?

As I make the turn east through the farm at Clashgour, I'm half expecting to be upbraided in the way that was so common before 2003 about my reckless endangerment of the farm's dogs, but they seem to be safely in their kennels, and there are no kids or sheep to be seen either. It's odd, though, how the old cringe abides, and a self-possessed gamekeeper can still get me feeling that I'm doing something ... if not illicit then not quit licit either. Hopefully, once a whole generation has grown up expecting access to moor, loch and hill, that attitude will just wither, but there will always be a trace of it in me.

* * *

The road out of the glen is a good one, doubtless built to get the guns in for the deer, and I pick up the pace, the smaller cogs on the cassette seeing the chain for the first time in a day as I pass Glasgow University's eccentric Clashgour tin hut bothy, which is used as a rough and ready base for expeditions by students into the wilds of the Black Mount. At this speed it's not long before I come to the end of the gravel road at Victoria Lodge and meet tarmac for the first time at a T-junction. It's the old road round the west edge of Loch Tulla and, in fact, just the latest iteration of one of the oldest roads in the Highlands – the great road from the west coast to the Lowlands through Glencoe. It was a track and then a drove road since before written records began, then became the basis for the military road from Stirling to Fort William, before being upgraded by Thomas Telford in the early 1800s. It is now part of the West Highland Way walking route.

I make a conscious effort to remind myself that I'll be on a public road for a bit, with the Highway Code and all that implies, and swing out right in the direction of Bridge of Orchy. I'm happy and relieved to have come through what I reckon will be one of the toughest bits of the journey, over wild country I don't know at all well, and I'm keen to share this feeling with the steady stream of walkers coming the other way. Hikers start to appear in groups of all colours and moods. All of them get a cheery hello and a ring of my big red bell, and most respond with a smile, or even a returned hello from the North Americans. But there are some truly downtrodden folk who you'd think were doing this as penance or at gunpoint, for all the pleasure on their faces. From their packs, I'd guess they're not trying to set any sort of endurance records, but they look like they've been at it for days on end without sleep. If I was going to make the effort to walk ninety-six miles from one town to another across wild ground, I'm not sure I would want the company of a whole lot of other people or to camp near anyone else, but maybe this is the first time they've done something like this and they're just gritting their teeth and ploughing on towards the train they've got booked in a couple of days' time.

I cross the stone arch of the Drochaid Tolaghan and sweep round to Inveroran, a place that is now all but forgotten but which was always at the centre of the droving trade. For centuries it was a 'stance', where cattle moving from as far afield as the Outer Hebrides on their way to market at Falkirk or Crieff Tryst would be allowed to rest and graze overnight. As the law came to recognise less and less the common nature of land – the right of anyone to move over it with their beasts – this was the first stance to have a fee levied for grazing and then to be enclosed, something that the drovers challenged in the High Court. To this day, there is a farm a bit further on near Bridge of Orchy where, as a result of this challenge, the tenancy agreement includes a duty to allow passing cattle to be stanced for a regulated fee.

From Inveroran, my route takes the tarmac road round to Bridge of Orchy and it's a real pleasure to hear the tyres' rough tread singing as I put the foot down a bit, motivated by the thought that I have definitely earned a burger and pint of beer, if any such thing can be procured in the village. It's sometimes hard to appreciate how primitive communications used to be in the Highlands, but this very road was described in a 1900 cycling guide as 'a bad road. From Tyndrum to Inveroran the surface is poor – in fact very stony – thereafter the road becomes much worse.' Now the modern tarmac is speeding me towards a pint in Bridge of Orchy.

Many writers have noted that Highland transport used to float on alcohol, from the drovers with their horns filled with whisky, to the soldiers who built the military roads and had unofficial licence to brew their own beer in their 'hutts', to the toll collectors on the turnpike roads who, to a man, doubled as whisky merchants. Ours has always been rough country to cross and even in summer the weather isn't always clement, so a little something to dull the pain has doubtless always been welcome, if not a necessity. I really cannot see any reason to break with tradition now.

The River Orchy looks lively as I cross the bridge and follow my nose towards the hotel that seems to be the only saloon in town. There doesn't appear to be anything in the way of cycle racks outside but I'm now starving and starting to fantasise about beer so I just prop the bike and trailer in front of the hotel and sling on the cable lock. The first thing I do on entering the hotel is to head to the gents for a quick wash. I'm acutely aware that I've been cycling for a day now and slept rough, so a quick sluice in hot water is going to be welcomed by all.

I actually feel a bit claustrophobic being indoors and I'm delighted to notice a balcony off the main bar where I can get a seat in the fresh air. I'm still worried about my animal smell, but the Polish waitress is charm personified. I pass the time before my pint of IPA and venison burger arrive chatting with a couple from Bolton on the next table. They've certainly got the right idea, doing the West Highland Way in ten easy chunks with light packs and staying in hotels and bunkhouses. They ask where I'm off to and there's something that holds me back from saying 'Findhorn' in case I jinx the trip. I don't know where I'm off to, after all. It could be Findhorn, it could be the hospital if I get it wrong, so I just say Glen Lyon, which is where I'm hoping to camp tonight, and it turns out that the man ice-climbed on the hills above in his youth.

When the beer comes, it is astonishing. Cold enough to make my neck hurt and bitter enough to cut right through the grime and filth that seem to have impregnated mind and body alike. The burger is also brilliant and demolished along with a stack of oversized chips. Simple pleasures are always the best when you've been out of doors and I may not be ready for opera or dainty soufflés for a while.

Outside, I give the bike a quick check over before setting off. The rear brake blocks look to be wearing quickly, which is a bit of a worry but not the end of the world as most of the braking is done on the front disc brake. Still, it's good to have a rear brake on the downhills to keep the trailer from trying to come round to the front and jack-knifing the whole arrangement. Rim brakes do pick up a lot of grit on rough country and these hydraulic ones are so powerful that this grit becomes a very effective abrasive for the brake pads. It's nothing to worry about for now and I set off, slightly giddy from the beer, across the main road when a gap in the incomprehensibly fast traffic presents itself.

An underpass gets you to the other side of the railway tracks and it's known as a place for mountain bikers on the West Highland Way to show off by riding the stairs. I'm not sure I've got what it takes to do that at the best of times, but with a trailer full of kit there's no way I'm even thinking about it. I dismount and accept the mild humiliation of bang-bang-banging the whole lot down and up the stairs, to the amusement of the passing walkers. They're laughing now, but I can probably cover three times as much ground as them outwith this staircase.

From here, I'm following the walkers' path that is actually the course of the eighteenth-century British military road, and even though it is quite badly degraded by years of neglect and scree falling from the slopes of Ben Dorrain towering above, it's hard not to feel the presence of the squads of redcoats that built it and travelled over it on their way from Stirling to Fort William. After the union of 1707 and the Jacobite uprising of 1715 it became clear to the government in London that the road network in the Highlands was ill-suited to their purposes. Ill-suited because it was virtually non-existent, consisting of vague drove-roads devoid of bridges, crossing wild high ground and only really defined by the hooves of the cattle driven over them. They sent the Irishman General George Wade to investigate the best way to proceed. He was experienced in warfare in wild country (and also the MP for Bath) and his 1724 report proposed appointing Protestant magistrates and keeping a close eye on a select group of Catholics in order to favour the establishment of 'an order in those Parts and Reducing the Highlanders to a more due submission to Your Majesty's Government'.

Barely mentioned in the report, possibly because it was so obvious, was the need to build a network of roads; partly so that garrisoned troops could back up the magistrates, and, equally importantly, so that Highland recruits to the new British army could be moved south. Work on the network began in 1725 with the Fort William to Fort Augustus road, and the project continued into the 1780s. This stretch was built in 1751.

No one had ever tried to make roads through the Highlands before. The army engineers had to invent their own techniques and learn from their failures. Almost all of the roads were eventually realigned from their original courses and most of the early bridges were washed away in winter floods. Our uplands were noted at the time to be 'still more impracticable from the want of Roads, Bridges and from the Excessive Rains that almost continually fall in those parts; which, by nature and constant use, become habitual to the Natives, but very difficultly supported by the Regular Troops'. In order to overcome the reluctance of soldiers to serve in the roadmaking battalions, those working with pick and shovel were paid at twice their normal daily rate and allowed to brew their own beer, something which the Exchequer took exception to but which was eventually allowed due to the 'heavy land carriage' for getting beer from the Lowlands to the men. In a nice echo of my own self-sufficient approach to the vagaries of Highland hospitality, Wade noted that 'there is so great a scarcity in this barren country that I am obliged to bring my biscuit, cheese etc. from Edinburgh by land carriage'.

It's difficult now to imagine how hard the work would have been, sleeping in tents or rough 'hutts', starting at four o'clock each morning to move and break boulders with crowbars and hammers while wearing woollen clothes and leather-soled shoes. The midges alone must have been murder. Despite this, each man made about a yard and a half of road, sixteen feet wide, across the intractable bogs and moors every day, at a cost of about a £100 per mile. Many of these roads can still be found where they haven't been obliterated by tarmac. It is hard to compare prices with the early eighteenth century, but each mile of the A9 dual carriageway being built as I write costs around £37 million. Using a private soldier's wages as the measure of inflation, this figure is about two hundred times the cost of the Wade roads.

✳ ✳ ✳

The West Highland Way walkers I encounter coming up the glen as I head down to my turn are a bit more cheerful than the morose, cagoule-draped squadrons at Inveroran, including a bunch of raucous Spaniards, and I get caught up in their mood, finally shaking off the last shadow of the panic from the head of Glen Kinglass.

The navigation for finding my turn off the main drag couldn't be much simpler, as it's the site of one of the classic picture postcards of the region. Apart from the West Highland Way and the main road, the West Highland Railway also makes its way through Glen Orchy, with a famous view where the railway, high on a viaduct, makes a sweeping turn as it crosses the Allt Kinglass, which runs down Glen Auch. That's attractive enough as a scene, but there's the additional element that the entrance to Glen Auch is guarded by a pair of handsome mountains – Ben Dorrain, which looks almost perfectly conical, and the craggy buttresses of Beinn a' Chaisteil, which has the look of a fortress about it. A simple stone bridge over the river, which sadly isn't a Wade original, and then it's a clear left turn to the north-east, which will leave the relatively busy world of Glen Orchy and the west coast behind. At the top of the glen, I'll actually cross the east–west watershed and enter into what is one of the highest and wildest parts of Tayside, despite being only a few kilometres from the Atlantic.

The estate whose track I'll be following has the particularity that the upland farming subsidies paid to it are publicly known, having been detailed in the estate agent's brochure when the estate was sold in 2012. In the previous year, they amounted to £696,909, which would quickly offset the asking price of eleven and a half million. Quite who receives these funds now is anybody's guess, the estate being officially owned by a company called, at the time of my expedition, Auch Farming Vehicle Ltd, whose registered headquarters was an accountant's office in Wigan. It will be interesting to see on the traverse across the estate quite what it is we're getting for seven hundred grand. Maybe there will be a free cocktail bar with a relaxed dress code at the top of the climb. I hope so anyway.

It's clear from the map that, whatever Auch estate spends its money on, it isn't bridges. The track meanders about on either side of the river, crossing it and its tributaries between ten and twenty times in the space of one hundred and fifty metres' climb, but apart from the bridge I just crossed, all the other crossings are fords. My beach shoes are going to have to earn their keep on the way to the top.

The first crossing may have benefitted from some of those farming subsidies as it's a proper concrete apron sunk into the river bed and broad enough that it's washed by just a couple of inches of water. It almost feels like cheating to roll across it at speed and hear the hiss of the spray against the mudguards. A good estate road leads up and under the railway viaduct on a perfect gradient that just lets me amble along without having to drop into first gear. Going under the railway feels like passing through a portal, though up close the concrete construction is disappointing and slightly shabby.

Glen Auch is pleasant enough but apart from the shooting it's obvious that the other activity is sheep. I can't see any at the moment, but the grass on the hillsides is cropped close between the banks of bracken to reveal the rocks in places, and I can smell their unmistakeable odour. I don't know any better word for that than the north-east 'strang'. It's like a mixture of urine and sweat had been left to go stale.

A couple of kilometres up the glen, the river crossings begin in earnest. It may be called an *allt* – a burn – but it most certainly is a river, and the fords are wild ones. There's a proper childish pleasure to be had from riding a bicycle through a river, only multiplied by knowing that I've got all my kit and rations in a waterproof roll-top bag in the trailer behind. For the most part, riding a bike over uncertain ground is a question of letting it do whatever it wants underneath you, not reacting to it, relaxing and just letting it roll over whatever's in the way at a decent pace. Still, I can't quite stop myself peering forward at the river bed, trying to pick out a line and estimate depth. I wouldn't want to ride in, only to find I need a snorkel, and it's amazing quite how dense and clingy water is once you cycle into any depth of it.

I love the sound that bike wheels make as they go into a river and the ephemeral, hemispherical bow wave thrown up and forward in front of the tyre like delicately blown glass. There's an odd, high-pitched ringing that reminds me of the energy crammed into bicycle wheels in the compressed air of the inner tube, and the screaming tension in the thirty-six stainless steel wires that hold the rim in its circular orbit around the hub. When I did a wheel-building course, we had to cut up the wheels we'd built through the day rather than taking them apart again, and the noise when the spokes of a properly tightened wheel are cut is an impressive indication of the perfectly balanced strain they are under.

A couple of times the water is narrower and deeper and I can't quite bring myself to ride into it. There's no shame in getting off and pushing, and there's yet another childish pleasure in wading through a Highland burn. I can't help but think of my childhood summer holidays building dams on burns just like this, wearing a pair of plastic sandals to keep my feet safe from the rocks. If there's any aspect of cycling – from buying bikes to riding them, fixing them and falling off them – that *doesn't* put you in mind of your childhood, I've yet to figure out what it is.

When I planned this trip, I had no real idea what the terrain would be like or how quickly I could get across it. I used my experience of the classic coast-to-coast, and my natural desire to linger and mooch around my country, to come up with a figure of fifty-five kilometres a day. A road cyclist would barely be warmed up after that distance, and a long-distance Audax rider wouldn't even notice it, but it's a decent ride on a mountain bike and more than that with camping gear and trailer wrestling with the rear axle.

From the bothy, if you ride fifty-five kilometres the way I'm going, you come to one of the most extraordinary sites I have ever encountered, high up in Gleann Cailliche, above the north shore of Glen Lyon. The Tigh nam Bodach – the Old Man's House – may be the oldest continuously operated shrine on our island, a turf and stone hut about the size of a large bathtub and home to a family of river-worn stones the size and shape of bowling pins. They represent Bodach, the old man, Cailleach, his wife, and their children. It's Bodach's house but it is Cailleach who's in charge of fertility, and it is her that was traditionally worshipped by local people who would bring her and her family out of the hut for Beltane in the springtime and back in for Samhain before the snows. This ceremony still happens here, in the absolute wilds, every year. I think it would be rude to enquire who actually does the shifting, and the air of mystery and power about the place is quite tangible. My plan is to camp at a respectable distance from the Tigh and see if Cailleach or Bodach won't visit my dreams.

As I climb, the river narrows and the crossings become ever shallower and more perfunctory until eventually they peter out and I'm left winding up the glen in solitude and calm. But I can feel the morning's hard work in my shoulders and legs now, and it's a great relief to cross a wooden bridge, with steel cages of boulders as parapets, over the Allt Tarabhan and realise that I'm now in the catchment of the Tay. Because the estate has land on both sides of the watershed, the sale brochure boasted that it has 'the unusual distinction of providing anglers with the opportunity to catch, on a single estate, salmon that entered the estate from both the east and west coasts'. On a west-to-east journey, that means it's all downhill from here, on average. Or something. It's good anyway, and another milestone.

I can just see Loch Lyon down below and the Breadalbane hills behind, their bare flanks ribbed like a whale's throat. The shore of the loch is a pale buff rocky band where the hydroelectric scheme has sent the water level up and down, drowning the land plants and drying out the aquatic ones.

After the effort of the climb comes the reward of the descent, and I luxuriate in the feel of the coursing air rippling my windproof shirt and the sound of the chain stepping down the cassette onto the small cogs on the run down to the lochside. I can hear the trailer banging about from side to side behind me, but at this kind of speed the bike's wheels have so much gyroscopic stability that it makes no difference. And anyway, as I sweep down, I realise I'm past caring. This morning's drama and exertion are starting to catch up with me, which is something I'd better keep an eye on. There's no lifeguard to drag me out if I miss the turn and ride into the loch.

Once you have seen the characteristic figure-of-eight shape of Cailleach, you start to spot it in stone all over Highland Perthshire. She and her man stand proudly on top of the entry pillars to Fortingall Old Kirk at the entrance to Glen Lyon, in a clear show of just which deity is really in charge round here – a sentence I hope is sufficiently ambiguous to avoid offence. Up here at the head of Glen Lyon, a stone propped by the lochside edge of the track catches my eye: another Cailleach someone has seen fit to secure by the wayside, maybe taken from a shrine flooded when the loch was dammed.

The undulating estate track round the north shore of the loch is starting to reveal a simple fact that shouldn't really come as a surprise: I'm quite tired. I'm an office drone who's been hacking a heavy and at times not entirely practical vehicle over rough ground all day. Most of my everyday cycling involves going to work or the shops, nothing like this, and I'm starting to have fond thoughts of a lie-down and a cup of tea. The Tigh nam Bodach isn't quite on my route – it's a couple of kilometres and maybe twenty metres above the junction where I could turn – and my will to cycle fades as I come round the bluff and get sight of the wide strath of Gleann Meurain, glowing in the evening sun. There is one more ford to be ridden, and the effort of changing my shoes yet again tips the decision. I will cross the Allt Meurain and camp on the opposite bank at Eilean Riabhach.

Quite why it's called 'speckled island' I do not know, but there is level ground and good water and even a half-ruined sheep fank to put my stuff on. I'm close enough to the Tigh to pick up the vibes and definitely in Cailleach country, so this is quite far enough for one day. The river is deep but the bed is stable and after a brief churning of the cranks under the water I'm hauling up onto the gravel bank and casting an eye around for the best place to sling the tent.

* * *

I suppose that there must have been classes and courses for learning to camp when I was young but I never took any of them. I'm the kind of person who slopes off into the hills alone or with a couple of friends, rather than joining the Scouts. Everything I know about camping I've learned by getting it wrong myself. The worst thing I've done so far is to underestimate the capacity of the sky over Skye to hold water. The result was that I got stranded on the wrong side of what had seemed like an innocuous burn, which overnight turned into a raging cataract that had the audacity to climb into our sleeping bags and slap us awake at three in the morning. That is not a mistake I'm ever keen to repeat so I'm careful to have a look at the height of the bank on this side of the river as well as the far side. I've got at least a metre drop to the water and the bank on the far side is much less steep, so I reckon that if the rain does come on, the flood will be on the other side.

The other matter is comfort – it's easy to put the tent up somewhere only to find that when you lie down you've got a hump under your midriff. The important thing is to actually lie down and find out if it's comfortable or not. It doesn't take too long to find a good spot amongst the clumps of reeds and break out my tent for the first time.

It's a featherweight one-person that I bought second-hand. You know straightaway when a piece of kit has been designed and made by people who intend to actually use their own product. This one is a slick delight, enthusiastically cooperating in going from a snugly rolled pack to a perfectly pitched shelter with no drama. You can tell when a tent's pitched properly by pinging the top sheet. This one rings like a drum, the skin held taut by the sparse but carefully crafted guy strings. Once the tent's up, what had just been a heap of discarded kit, a bicycle and a trailer is magically transformed into a campsite that becomes home. The whole thing is complete when I plant the small Lion Rampant flag off the trailer at the entrance to the tent, making it my castle.

I can't get over the feeling that I'm filthy and that I stink. There's no one around at all to be bothered about that but it's hard to shake off the habits that make urban living tolerable. The only place to wash is in the river, and just like any Westerner used to bathrooms and taps, I can never quite believe how inaccessible water in rivers is. It's always far lower than I expect and the stones on the riverbank never quite seem to have been properly installed to allow easy access. And, in this quite treeless country, there's no privacy either. Any passing deerstalker on the hill may well be treated to the sight of my milky-white backside getting a good wash and dry. But needs must, and in the water I let the salt crust wash away towards distant Dundee and the chill seep into my body and skull. Propped against the tumbledown sheep fank, the bike makes a perfect drying rack for my towel. Everything has to have at least two uses, and that includes the bike.

I need a lie-down and now that I'm clean and changed into long trousers and a long-sleeved top for the inevitable midge madness to come, I crawl into the tent as if it was a Neolithic chamber, a warmly lit womb to hide from the almost overwhelming landscape of tall, bare-scraped hills and deep black water all around. With the blow-up mat under the sleeping bag it is surprisingly cosy, and I drift off for a short but very deep and very satisfying sleep, from which I wake calm and oddly content to be here, absolutely alone in the heart of my country.

There being no one to talk to and no distractions from the absolute essentials of life, I set about feeding myself and making myself as comfortable as I can. The stove goes on to heat, the pasta and sauce come out of the day's ration bag, and the remaining third of the bottle of wine comes out from hiding. The bike, the tent, the big pink roll-top bag and the upturned trailer – transformed into a settee by the addition of the sleeping mat – form my living room tonight. Everything I have and everything I need is here. While the water heats there is nothing to do but contemplate the clouds passing over the flanks of the mountains and consider the folk who lived here and worshipped Bodach and Cailleach.

The isolation of the place is only underlined by the passing of a big four-by-four wagon, driven hard through the ford by an impassive estate worker going home for his tea, which I decide he's going to eat in front of the television. I raise my hand to him, but he doesn't see it or maybe considers travellers to be beneath greeting.

It may be isolated now, but this was for some time a major crossroads in the transport network of the country, where the road I'm riding crossed the road from the far north-west. It went over Rannoch Moor and up into this glen before heading south over Glen Lochay. In 1749, some cattle were reived from Tummel Bridge and soldiers despatched to this exact spot to intercept them on the 'Skye road'. This same route was surveyed but then abandoned by Telford in the third great era of way-making as a possible route from Fort William to Perth, a decision which means that two hundred years later I'm not camped beside a busy A-road but a humble estate track in near total silence and absolute solitude.

My mood of mellow contemplation is deepened by the food and wine. I enter a kind of hypnotic reverie, where the slopes of Beinn Sheasgarnich, on the other side of Loch Lyon, become my television screen. With the sun starting to set and the clouds drifting gently by, the hillside is wrapped in glowing orange tiger-stripes as the shadows of the clouds are beamed down to earth. The raking light only highlights the deep gullies carved into the landscape, but the overall effect is magical and it's only the campsite itself quickly falling into shadow that brings me round from my absorption. As the temperature drops, I decide that a stroll to loosen off my muscles might be a good idea.

Heading up the track I'll be taking tomorrow brings me to a place where the peat bog is giving up the stumps of mature trees with trunks a good thirty centimetres across. The treeline here is around five hundred metres and I'm below that but above the usual limit for commercial planting of three hundred and fifty metres. The trees could be as old as the Bronze Age and they speak of a glen with a completely different look and likely a very different climate. It isn't hard at all to look up from the peat hag, where the stumps sit surrounded by bog cotton, to the surrounding hills and to imagine mature woods climbing up above the ancient drove road, now below the surface of the loch.

One of the reasons that relatively few of us venture out across the wild country is the Highland midge. A lot of research has been done on this tiny biting fly over the years and a number of products have emerged to keep it at bay to some extent, but no solution has ever been found that allows human beings to be outdoors between May and September without getting bitten. Whether they emerge or not is down to a complex set of variables, but the most important ones are humidity, light intensity and wind speed. The midge is tiny. It has a huge surface area for its volume and, incredibly, it is in danger of desiccating the moment it leaves the famously damp land on which it breeds and rests. So unless the humidity is high enough, the light low enough and the wind gentle, they stay put. But when the right conditions do come about, they can emerge and locate a suitable warm-blooded target with a precision and persistence that would do credit to the most advanced military drones.

Now the midges are getting to the point where I have to put on my head net, and there's just no way that admiring the country through a fine, black nylon mesh is any equal to seeing it with the naked eye. The insects have won and I retreat to the tent for a sleep that I can feel will be every bit as deep and satisfying as my pre-dinner nap earlier on.

I don't normally engage in mystical thought, being more of a scientific and empirical bent, but I've always felt drawn to Glen Lyon since the first time I heard about it and looked it up on a map. The Tigh nam Bodach and the Fortingall Yew at the entrance to the glen are both utterly extraordinary, commanding my respect in a way that few human beings do. The doyenne of mountain writing, Nan Shepherd, had it that 'no one knows the mountain completely who has not slept on it'. I'm not ashamed to say that I'm keen to see what Bodach or Cailleach has to say in my dreams tonight, even if I'm not quite as close to their house as I had hoped.

My calm is broken by the intrusion of a mundane but inescapable concern and, in the middle of one of the wilder tracts of land available, I find myself forced by my own nagging mind to put the padlock and cable on the bike. There is no one for miles in any direction, but I just can't quite bring myself to leave the bike unsecured. Many of the concerns and worries of city life are struggling to keep up with my progress into the wilderness, but personal hygiene and fear of thieves both seem to be managing fine.

Back in the tent I lay my head down on the rolled-up fleece that serves as a pillow and sleep comes at me with the speed and force of a mainline train going through a quiet rural station.

When I wake it's because I need a pee and it's just after four in the morning. There's always a delicate internal negotiation with these things when you're camping because the effort of sitting up and unzipping tent flaps, and generally thrashing about in the half dark, is so much greater than in your own house, as is the contrast in temperature between your warm bag and the outside air only an arm's length away. The internal negotiation proceeds for a few moments before definitively coming down on the side of getting up and taking a short stroll away from the tent. As I unzip the outer flysheet I change my mind as what appears to be a whole galaxy of black anti-stars is revealed silhouetted against the midnight blue of the sky. If I go out there, I am going to be eaten down to the bone by the thickest cloud of midges I have ever seen, and which has clearly been gathered from the entire strath by the sweet perfume of my slumbering body. The inner lining of the tent has done its job perfectly as I haven't a bite on me, and I quickly zip it shut again to stem the onslaught of microscopic airborne zombies.

There's only one solution to the urgent pressure in my bladder given that the outside air is going to be hostile until the sun comes up, and it's the kind of filthy compromise you get up to when you're camping. The plastic lemonade bottle that I had decanted my wine into does just fine, and afterwards I put the top on tight and prop it in the far corner of the tent to avoid a midge invasion. That's not something I'd do at home, but the normal rules are starting to wear a bit thin. Only two generations back nobody in my family had an inside lavatory and no one was squeamish about having a chamber pot under the bed. I can feel myself slipping back in time as I push forward through the hills.

Three

Rannoch

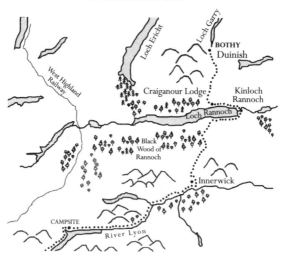

As my eyes begin to see the greenish-yellow glow inside the tent I know that Bodach hasn't joined me in a dream. Perhaps he and his wife felt snubbed that I didn't go the extra mile to camp with them, or maybe the profound and restful night's sleep I just had was their gift. Whatever the truth of it, by seven I'm ready to get up and put the kettle on for coffee and breakfast. The hills around me are bursting with green but oddly subdued in the flat morning light compared to last evening's orange glow, still vivid in my mind.

Although this is only my second morning on the trip, my routine is already becoming reflex. Changing out of my trail pyjamas – a thermal top and a pair of fleecy tartan trews – fetching water from the river and getting the stove lit. Dosing out a packet of freeze-dried cappuccino and topping up the taste and caffeine with a couple of spoons of granules. Each day's rations are in a labelled zip-lock bag; the breakfast is the same each day, the lunch is different and the dinner is always pasta – except for tonight. If all goes to plan, tonight will be a midway point of the journey and to mark that Nathalie will be meeting me at a bothy in the high, wild country between Loch Rannoch and Loch Garry. That's part of the deal that has allowed me to take off on my own, and a prospect that will draw me on all day. I'm an introvert by nature – profoundly comfortable in my own company – but there's so much to tell and the grand solitude of my country is almost overwhelming my capacity to be alone.

My ration plan recognises the importance of this evening and I've treated myself to a freeze-dried wild mushroom risotto. It would be uncivilised to have risotto without cheese, and packed away amongst today's rations is a tightly knotted plastic bag of grated Gran Padano cheese. I used to use Parmesan until I saw some Italian friends using the cheaper stuff; a blind taste test proved that I couldn't tell the difference once it was stirred into food. I think I'd be a lot more content if I'd been equally insistent on choosing other things in my life so empirically.

With the coffee and suitably spiced beans and sausage inside me, it's time to strike the tent, wash the dishes and pack the trailer. I'll need to take a private moment before I get going too. It's certainly one of the trickier bits of wild camping and, I'm pretty sure, something that puts lots of people off who otherwise might be keener. Westerners are so used to sitting on flush toilets that anything else feels distinctly unnatural, taboo even. But there is a simple code that can be followed and with a bit of practice it becomes quick and easy to dig a small hole somewhere discreet and put the turf back so that it's almost impossible anyone will ever know or notice. This is what many people in the world do every morning, after all, and if they can then so can we.

What is critical is cleanliness, though, and I have a good wash in the river before hitching the trailer up, slinging on my backpack and heading up to the deserted T-junction with the estate road that will lead me down to the tarmac at Pubil. This is a fossilised remnant of the original junction between the Skye Road and the road that ran the length of the glen. The original may have been here or may now be submerged, but this is its echo and I pull out onto the deserted track only when there is a safe gap in the ghostly traffic.

An optimism comes to the cycling now, not just from my fresh legs but from knowing that gravity is, on balance, on my side for the next hour. The track oscillates a bit but it has to be flat overall along the length of the loch, then a steady drop down the glen to Innerwick, where I'll turn north into the hills again for the steepest climb of the journey. For now, the weather's good, my belly's full and I'm confident that the day will yield memories and sensations beyond the ordinary. The Gaick Pass through the southern Cairngorms is on my mind but that's a matter for tomorrow. Today, I'm content to turn the cranks over knowing that I'm dropping down into one of the most alluring glens I know. That tranquil confidence is slightly eroded by the soft chirping noise coming from my chain, and by the constant tension between my desire to lose myself in the landscape and the need to pay attention to the practical elements of travelling by bicycle.

Like almost every bicycle now, the one I'm using is based on the safety bicycle pattern that became common in the 1880s. It is relatively safe compared to its penny-farthing forerunners because the rider sits back and pedals a small rear wheel through a crank and chain rather than being perched above an enormous front wheel; an arrangement that makes a trip over the handlebars a near certainty at some point. The problem has always been how to transmit the energy from the cranks to the wheel in a way that is cheap, light and long-lasting. The steel chain is cheap and not too heavy but it certainly isn't fuss-free or long-lasting. I've worn out good chains in six weeks commuting to work before now, and if you don't oil them they soon turn bright orange and sing like a whole aviary of canaries. Yesterday's constant river crossings and peat bogs have stripped my chain of all its lubrication, leaving it in danger of rusting and seizing, robbing me of energy that should be going into propulsion rather than sound effects.

There are many and varied systems for power transmission in bicycles as well as for gearing. We're at the point now where the problem may have been solved definitively by sealed gearboxes – mounted either in the rear hub or in the frame in front of the cranks – in combination with a toothed drive belt made of Kevlar. These systems have two drawbacks: they're expensive at best and extortionate at worst, and if they *do* go wrong you can't fix them in the field.

I'm using a conventional chain and derailleur system. It's complex, a bit fragile and exposed to the elements, but it's also cheap, light and can often be sorted on the go with simple tools. In that regard it's just like the spirit stove. If you're going to operate independently you need to have kit that you understand, have full access to and can repair if the need arises. The complex, the unknown and the inaccessible, no matter how superficially attractive, are not your friends. And if things can have more than one use, so much the better. Another good idea is to carry oil when you're cycling in the wilderness, but unfortunately that seems to be something that slipped off my logistical planning grid, such as it was.

About halfway along the loch another note joins the clean, vegetal smell of the grassy moorland either side of me. My own smell may not be too fragrant after a couple of nights roughing it, but it is surely nothing compared to this; acrid, pungent and sweet all at once and immediately recognisable as the smell of death. I can't see anything and it's another twenty metres before I crest a slight rise to be confronted with the rictus grin on the skull of a carcass sprawled on the track. It's a blackface ewe, I think, but it's hard to tell as something has eaten its eyes and the skin off its head, leaving a grinning, stinking ovine demon.

The estate worker who passed my campsite last night must have seen it as there is no other road to take round here, but I guess maybe they're just left to rot or be scavenged by ravens and eagles, if there are any – I haven't seen a bird bigger than a meadow pipit since the falcon at the head of Glen Kinglass. Even breathing through my mouth the stench makes me gag and underlines the sense of hills that were alive once but are now scoured and spurned. Anyway, the head still has a tag in each ear so I'm sure it will be properly accounted for in some distant office.

The north side of Loch Lyon is a bleak bank of rough grassland, stripped to the bone by sheep and deer, but halfway along there's a fold in the ground where the steep banks have saved the land from these hungry beasts. If you were making determined progress on a bike here, you could easily miss it, rattling over the creosote-scented timbers of the bridge without noticing the Eas Eoghannan flowing in the gorge beneath you. It's a snaking oasis of lush vegetation and mature but scrubby trees – birch, rowan and alder – carved by a stream bouncing merrily down a series of steps in the rock and through chutes and channels it has carved in the layered stone and polished like marble over thousands of years. Downstream from the bridge, the burn tips off into the void and plunges into an arm of the loch tens of metres below. Upstream is a perfect pool, just wide and deep enough to swim in, fed with lightly peated water through a rippled spout, the bottom covered in multi-coloured, apple-sized stones. If I hadn't an appointment tonight, I'd be very tempted to slip in for a dip, but after clambering back up the bank, and a moment propped against the parapet, I shove off and in a second or two the very idea that this region could be sheltered and welcoming is wholly lost and gone as I strike out across the bare hill.

The track runs by the lochside but rises a hundred metres above the dam at the eastern end of the loch and drops one hundred and fifty on the other side to the hamlet of Pubil. It's a bit of a drag to the summit, but another delight to give the bike its head on the descent, going hard on the front brake on each switchback and trusting the tyres and suspension to deal with the weight of the trailer behind. There's a closed gate at the bottom and, once through, it's just natural and right to demonstrate viscerally what the front brake just did – dissipate all the energy I put into the climb and then some – by licking a finger and touching it on the steel disc for the satisfying hiss of boiling spittle.

Looking round, the memory of the vista of the glen from the side of the loch is swept away by the looming, and slightly grubby, Lubreoch Dam. It's part of the Breadalbane hydroelectric complex, an astonishing feat not just of engineering but of political will. It is composed of a vast web of dams, turbines, aqueducts and, most impressively of all, tunnels dug through the solid rock of the mountains in the 1950s. The intention behind it was first to provide a stable source of cheap electricity to the cities, but also to electrify the glens around the complex which still ran on coal and paraffin. Even then there was still an assumption that Highlanders were simple creatures with no need of modern convenience, and the head of the National Trust even went as far as to mock the project, which he thought to be disfiguring the landscape and disturbing the salmon, by suggesting that they were 'sending out little expeditionary forces to sell in the remote West Highland glens the idea that they must have electric cookers' – something that now sounds both remarkably patronising and short-sighted.

The drive for the project came from a remarkable visionary: Tom Johnston. He had been an energetic and interventionist Secretary of State during the Second World War whose every action during that conflict was intended to also improve the country afterwards. In due course, having resigned as an MP at the end of the war, he became a sort of governor-general, appointed simultaneously as the head of the Hydro Board, the Tourist Board and the Forestry Commission. This situation came about after a visit to Inverness from the then Chancellor of the Exchequer, Hugh Dalton, who declared that 'the Highlands must be led into a better future not by the private hand of Adam Smith but by the visible public hand of the Labour Party'.

The 1950s were an austere time in a United Kingdom still in the shadow of the war. Construction of the Breadalbane scheme was begun with food rationing still in place. It was a genuine struggle for the nation to find the labour and materials to build the dams – to the extent that one fifth of the concrete at Lubreoch consists of fly ash from coal power stations, meaning that, rather deliciously, this solidly built renewable energy infrastructure literally rests on the ashes of the fossil fuel industry.

The men who built the dams and tunnels worked in conditions that wouldn't have looked out of place in the Klondike Gold Rush, their rustic labour camps notorious for drinking, fighting and thieving. At least they'd have got away from the midges while they were tunnelling, but it is almost impossible to imagine either their presence or the optimism and energy of that era now that the dam itself has blackened with lichen and settled into the wild landscape.

From the dam, in the space of a minute or two, I drop from wilderness to country with a sort of scrappy, end of the line, semi-industrial look. It feels a bit like coming back to earth from orbit in the hills behind, and it's only once I'm on the tarmac road that the feeling recedes as I begin to follow the wildly beautiful River Lyon. Maybe it's in recognition of this beauty that the sun comes out from behind the morning's low cloud to pick out the trout rising through what looks like light ale.

It takes a certain unwelcome effort to work it out, but this is definitely a Saturday morning. The weather is perfect and yet there is no one about. Not a soul. I scan the banks of the river for fishermen, and the hillsides for walkers, but neither is showing well. This glen is remote in the sense that it's two hours' drive from Perth, but it's not the end of the world, and it is quite literally so magnificent that I can't stop myself smiling. Maybe people don't know that they have the right to come here, to camp and to kayak on the lochs and rivers as long as no harm is done? Surely there can't be many other countries in the world where, on a sunny weekend morning only a couple of hours from a city, brown trout rise on one of the most beautiful rivers in existence unmolested by a single angler? As far as I know, the wild trout belong to whoever is fly enough to catch them.

Cruising down the glen with my new friends gravity and tarmac, it seems the big dam at Pubil isn't the only power-plant in the glen. Various sluices, tunnels and access tracks lacing up the slopes come and go from view. The almost imperceptible electrical hum feels oddly complementary to the magical power I've felt here, just like on Iona, in ways I can't challenge empirically and which still sit uneasily with the rational, scientific part of me. There's just something about the way the beauty of Glen Lyon is tucked away in the heart of the country behind its steep walls and the bends of its own snaking curve, like a boudoir in a grim tower house, that makes it feel like a natural haven and last resort. I'll be sad to leave it when I turn for the north.

As I pass the turn-off to the seat of the historical and current owners, Meggernie Castle, I'm still in a reverie over the power of the now well-wooded landscape undisturbed by anything so vulgar as a car when a brown hare jacks out of a hedgerow and into the roadway on its absurd back legs. It's not bothered about me at first but then it can't often have seen this much bike, luggage and cyclist bearing down on it at this time of the morning. As man and baggage train advance, it decides to shift along the road a bit to save any strife. That doesn't seem to work so it shifts a bit further and stops a second time, which again doesn't work as we're heading the same way. It breaks into a gentle trot down the road in that crazy, loping gait that hares have when they're at ease, like a clown car with square wheels, an impression only deepened by the big, floppy ears the hare is still holding upright.

On nice, smooth, downhill tarmac with twenty-odd kilos behind me I can easily go up through the gears. I slip the chain onto the big chain wheel for the first time in a while and put a bit of pressure on the pedals, feeling the rear axle tug on the trailer hitch. The hare responds with a faster, more fluid gait. I'm thinking that it'll get bored and dive off to one side or the other. But, instead of jinking sideways, it decides that straight-line speed is its ace. It isn't. I drop the chain into the smallest sprocket and follow, caught up – against my better judgement – in the absurdity of the moment. I'm close enough to see its ears pin back as it adopts the flat-out pace its legs were designed for and becomes a sinuous, pounding blur.

Anyone witnessing the scene would wonder what obscure hunting tradition could possibly involve the pursuit of such a creature by a grubby man on a ratty bicycle. The chase can't last, surely? We must be going thirty miles an hour now and I'm going to feel extremely guilty if the hare, as seems likely, blows a gasket and drops dead in mid-stride. My mum once chased a rabbit into a coma by mistake after she caught it eating her parsley. I'm not far off the heart attack stage myself, pedalling flat out in top gear, crouched down over the straight bars for speed and actually gaining on the poor beast. Things are getting a bit giddy as we swoop and swerve around the sweeping single-track road and I can feel the trailer starting to waggle and sway as our speed hits the safe limits for the load. Just then the hare thinks better of trying to run and pirouettes neatly back into the lush undergrowth.

I sit up off the bars and let the bike coast for a bit to get my breath back, relieved that my slightly unhinged pursuit of the poor animal has left us both unharmed. I'd be horrified to see anyone set out to chase a hare deliberately, but somehow I'd got sucked into it. It's a mad moment and I feel both curiosity and shame that I seem to have shuffled off my own standards so easily after a couple of nights in the wilds.

The glen is a bit more inhabited as I come down towards the hamlet of Bridge of Balgie and at long last I spot a few folk fishing by their riverside campsites. This is quite an idyllic setting and while there is no doubt I'll be back with a fishing rod some time, my main aim right now is to reach the café at the post office, well-known for its cakes. Cakes and coffee are the fuel of cyclists the world over and also the glue that binds us together. No group ride-out at any level other than professional racing is complete without an espresso and a fat slab of carrot cake, and although I couldn't be more alone I don't intend to pass up this perfect opportunity for a mid-morning stop.

* * *

Bridge of Balgie is at the junction of the road down the glen and another that crosses over the Ben Lawers massif from Loch Tay, climbing to five hundred and fifty metres in the process. This makes for a perfect circular training ride for road cyclists going up Loch Tay over the hills and back down Glen Lyon. On a beautiful summer morning like this I'm expecting the café to be clattering with the sound of impractical cycling shoes, but all twelve bike racks are empty when I arrive. They're the kind that cyclists call toast racks or wheel-benders, designed to take the front wheel wedged into an arrangement like a partly opened book. That's not ideal for anyone, but particularly not for me since I'll have to unhook the trailer if I don't want it sticking out into the road. There aren't any other cyclists in sight so I prop my bike and trailer across ten of the dozen places and make my way up to see what's on the menu.

Going into the café is almost overwhelming. The couple of days I've been outdoors have honed my antennae to the point where the noise of the machines, the smell of coffee and cleaning products and the simple presence of human beings is too much for comfort. It feels unnaturally enclosed too. Maybe this is what wild animals feel like when they stray through an open window into a house looking for food. I have to get a hold of myself a bit before a very pleasant lady carves me out a whole side of white chocolate and raspberry cake and promises to bring my latte outside. I'm keen to retreat from the humanity of the place.

I've no sooner sat down on the benches outside to listen in on the tourists on the other table than a flying circus of brand new mountain bikes pelts down and grinds to a halt in front of the racks I've just blocked with my shabby, homebrewed rig. I'll need to move it if I don't want ten mountain bikers on my case so I get up and make it as obvious that I can that I'm willing to shift my bike for them. Only Glaswegians could manage to be so totally friendly and so totally offhand in the same sentence as they tell me not to worry and proceed to prop their nice bikes all over the place, with some of them just pushed gently into the bracken. I'm intrigued by the eclectic mix of bikes and riders. There are girls on brand new, mid-range, chain-store mountain bikes, guys on brand-name mountain bikes and a lady on an ageing roadster, but although they're amiable enough they're not looking to talk to anyone outside their group. It looks like a bunch of friends have just decided to go for a ride over the Ben Lawers road and some have hired bikes for the outing. I hope they love it, get hooked and look further afield.

Just as I'm getting settled in front of my cake again, another cyclist rolls up to the café, and this time there's no doubt that he's a serious road cyclist, probably in race training. He's got metallic shades, aerodynamic covers on his shoes and a race team-branded shirt, all the gear. His cleated cycling shoes clatter as he duck-walks over the road with two empty *bidons* towards the nice lady from the café who's out clearing the table next to mine.

'Any chance you could fill up my water bottles?' he says, pouring some powder from a sachet into each one. A more cynical person than me would speculate on the performance-enhancing powers of the magic potion, and if it was me he was asking I might well direct him to the river for his water. But I guess she reckons there's the prospect of future business some time, or maybe she just sees the café as a social service as much as a business. It's not uncommon for cyclists of all stripes to be viewed as high-handed, entitled and arrogant, and I'm not convinced that asking for water in a remote café without buying a coffee or a postcard is going to help that. The two of us are no doubt from diametrically opposite arms of cycling's spiral galaxy, but I can't help feeling embarrassed on his behalf. He can't be skint, given the fancy bike he's riding. Maybe it's a one-off, maybe he's bought loads of stuff in the past here, but I'm left with the image of someone happy to travel through the country like it was a jaunt through hyperspace.

It occurs to me as I go back inside to settle up that there might be a can of three-in-one oil around the place for my chain. I'm pretty sure there's a flat above the café and every home has some sort of oil or lubricating spray. As expected, the lady isn't at all fazed by the request and goes off to hunt round the kitchen, though it turns out the only thing they've got that's remotely suitable is cooking oil. I've no idea how long that will last but it's better than nothing and I'm absolutely charmed by her generosity and ingenuity, two of my favourite things. I accept the offer and thank her profusely when she brings out a ramekin dish of sunflower oil. I'm glad it's not olive oil as I'm not sure I could have clarted that on a bicycle, and I'm even more relieved I haven't had to resort to margarine. The crushed end of a bracken stem has to serve as a sort of paint-brush to slather the vegetable oil as thickly as I can on a chain that is now bare metal, a shameful sight indeed for a careful cyclist. Dry chains wear out, rust, break and waste energy. Vegetable oil isn't ideal in any sense, but neither is a grating chain.

Any idea I had of a truly self-reliant journey ended with my first sip of beer at Bridge of Orchy, and I've no intention of trying to cross the Cairngorms with a squeaky chain, so there's no partic-ular shame in the text I send Nathalie on the one precious bar of phone signal in the glen. We're due to meet tonight but she won't have set off yet for the two- or three-hour drive to Dalnacardoch. Along with the oil bottle I forgot, I ask her to look out a spare pair of blocks for the rear brakes. Their fantastic hydraulic power, com-bined with the grit and filth of the rough country, have chewed up the blocks and quite possibly the alloy wheel rims quite badly. The brake lever is coming too close to the bar when it's squeezed and a fresh set of blocks will sort that nicely.

I hand the ramekin back to the café lady, along with yet another layer of thanks and praise for the coffee and cake. I'm still feeling faintly embarrassed for the young man on the fancy road bike, even though I've no idea if she was annoyed about him or not. I can't deny the responsibility I feel for him by dint of both of us being on bicycles despite not knowing him, where he came from or where he's going. The café lady asks me where I'm going, which puts me in a bit of a quandary. In the first place, I'm not actually sure the climb out of the glen over to Loch Rannoch is actually rideable with my load, and secondly, I haven't even the first vestige of a clue how to pronounce the name of the pass: the Lairig Ghallabhaich.

I grew up in Aberdeen and a regular source of entertainment was to wait for the Gaelic segment on the television news and laugh uproariously whenever the newsreader dropped a recognisably English word into the bulletin. How droll we must have been as we mocked the *telebhisean*. When I started hillwalking as a teenager, the issue became less clear-cut. There's no way you can discuss a route in the Cairngorms without using Gaelic. With a few exceptions, like the sharp peaks of Mount Keen and Vinegar Hill, the mountains don't have English names, so I learned to pronounce the common ones by imitation and took wild and shamefaced guesses at the gnomic names of the others. When I worked in France I took pride in learning their language to the full extent of my power to learn, so when I came back I could no longer deny feeling some shame that I didn't know what the Gaelic names on the map meant, let alone how to pronounce them. Little by little I learned the common colours and features of the land, such as burns, rivers and waterfalls, and the maps started to make a bit of sense.

Now I watch the Gaelic channel from time to time not to mock but to let the language wash over me and to listen out for the few words I do know, eagerly checking with the subtitles. We spent a very entertaining night in the pub a couple of years back with our most venerable Gaelic scholar after he asked if he could sit at our table. This ancient man, who spoke no English at all until he was five, proceeded to instil in me, with warmth and precision, a gentle shame that I had no Gaelic. One of these days I'll put in the week's work I'm told it takes to master the basics of the pronunciation. I may even attend an evening class, or maybe I'll even do something about getting the confidence to speak the Doric I can hear so clearly in my head but just can't bring myself to use unless I'm with another north-easter, I've got a drink in me, or both.

So instead of saying I'm heading over the Lairig Ghallabhaich I look the café lady in the eye with as much determination as I can and announce that I'm heading over the pass to Rannoch. 'Ah…' she says. 'What kind of bike are you on? It's a bit loose and rough these days.' It's not a question that I find easy to answer. I've no idea what kind of bike I've got. It's not a mountain bike because the frame is from a hybrid and the tyres are too thin. It's not a road bike because it's got flat bars, and it's not a tourer because it's got a fancy suspension fork. It's a mongrel, a bike like no other, a mountain tourer. Anyway, I doubt she's interested in that, she's just checking that I'm not planning to make a fool of myself on a skinny-tyred road bike, which plainly I'm not as I can make a fool of myself quite easily on the mountain tourer.

The other problem is that the stupid, vain and proud parts of me want to tell her that I've just ploughed the bike and wagon over a nameless morass out of Glen Kinglass and into Glen Lyon up Glen Auch. This is no time for bragging and I know that if I say where I've come from she'll ask where I'm headed next. The

Gaick Pass is looming in my mind, like the 'key-stane o' the brig' that the pursuing witches and demons dare not cross in 'Tam O'Shanter'. I'd be delighted to leave my own imps of self-doubt behind me in those wild hills, but that's not a subject for idle chatter in a café on a nice summer morning, so I nod my thanks and mutter something about having a look and managing, steel myself for the climb and head out onto the road for the last kilometre of tarmac in this glen.

The turn is easy enough to find, signposted directly opposite the austere but beautiful whitewashed kirk to which the pass led to from the villages of Rannoch. It's only eleven kilometres to the loch but the contour lines on the map gather over the start of the pass in an angry swarm, by far the steepest part of the whole journey. It is marked as a cart track throughout and I've high hopes that the surface will be more tractable than on the climb out of the Kinglass. It's time to shed a layer of clothing and slip the bike into its lowest gear before I leave the sealed road. I'll be taken aback if I can reach the top without a bit of pushing and I'm absolutely certain that second gear won't be needed until I hit the summit two hundred and seventy metres above me. Again, in the Tour de France scheme of things this might not even count as a climb, but it certainly does to me.

In the still midday air I start to sweat almost at once as I turn north through rough sheep pasture. The track branches and I take the right fork to follow the edge of a woodland plantation. It's at this point that the needles on all my meters swing over into the red. The surface of the track isn't too bad, for the simple reason that any round stone that comes loose from it will just have rolled to the bottom: this isn't steep, it's vertical. With each stroke of the pedals I can feel the tension in the top run of the chain and the weight of the trailer hanging on the back wheel. Pride kicks in, a voice whispering in my ear that I won't be beaten by a force as feeble as gravity.

The hardest bit of the climb out of Glen Kinglass was unrideable because the path was too rough to keep up any momentum, not because of the slope. Here the problem is two-fold: the steepness and the loose surface I'd just been warned about. Even with the additional weight of the trailer, the rear wheel is spinning up and spraying out a shower of gravel at any hint of power on the pedals, and for the first time I'm actually going to have to use some proper cycling techniques.

The thing with climbing is to have enough weight on the rear wheel to get traction and enough weight on the front to steer. If the front lifts off, you can't steer at all; and if the back spins, you've got no drive. A simultaneous absence of drive and direction isn't a state anyone wants to be in. The answer comes in two parts: first, you need to 'pedal in circles', with no discernible downstroke where the power is applied, just a constant torque throughout each rotation. Second, you need to get your weight forward and down, which means moving your arse up onto the nose of the saddle and your chest down towards the handlebars. This is a near-miraculous technique for cycling up the steepest slopes, but I'd be much keener on it if it didn't feel like being pinned down for a tentative proctological examination.

It is astonishing how slowly you can cycle when you have to, and in my lowest gear I'm only just above slow walking pace. Little by little, the floor of the glen drops below me, and the view opens up. The hills become bare and for the first time I'm really among that quintessence of the central and eastern Highlands: heather.

The pattern of burning and regrowth on the hillsides shows that I'm crossing my first grouse moor. It is a landscape as bleak to me as the hearts of the folk who have birds chased towards them for

target practice. I'm quite keen on hunting as a way of connect-
ing with my most basic instincts, but if what is killed isn't eaten I
don't think anyone involved can claim to be a gentleman. And the
effect on the land is shocking; scalped and bare. The sign down in
the glen spoke of three bloomeries along the way, a kind of early,
domestic-scale iron furnace used to make wrought iron from bog
iron ore and charcoal. They were built wherever the fuel was plen-
tiful, but you wouldn't get much charcoal off this hill now, the
trees never having recovered from the changing weather after the
Bronze Age, or the smelters or the sheep that followed, or the
grouse that followed them.

The land is magnificent in its scale but it is wounded. It really
would be better for all of us if we let a forest of birch, alder and
scrub oak grow back. Surely even the grouse shooters would
rather go on a pigeon shoot in a wood than crouch in a dugout to
knock down wave after wave of birds straight into landfill. And if
you don't believe they're usually thrown away, just ask yourself the
last time you saw grouse in the supermarket.

After half an hour or so of steady climbing, the gradient just
gets the better of me and it is time to dismount. The technique
now is what I call the 'Superman'. Not because I have any great
power, just because the best way to push up a really steep incline
is with both arms straight, head down and leaning steeply forward to transmit all the forces from the big leg muscles straight
through your locked arms, whose muscles are puny by compar-
ison. Progress is slow and the curse of the left-side pedal strikes
repeatedly. Bicycles, so imbued with effortless elegance when
you're riding them, become cussed, thrawn and angular when
pushed. The left-side pedal becomes a small, sharp demon and no
matter how many times it's spun forward out of the way, it creeps
back to have a bite at my shin.

The hard work sees the gradient slacken and me back on the bike, out of first gear and splashing through a small stream. The upper reach of the pass looks like someone has taken a gigantic lino cutter through the hill to form a great straight, gouged channel through which I get my first glimpse of what can only be the western edge of the Cairngorms massing as a dark band on the distant horizon. The notch of the pass forms a gunsight, the distant massif becomes the target and my mind becomes the bullet, fired out towards what is the central problem of any coast-to-coast ride: there are only a few ways through the Cairngorms that are practical on a bicycle. A handful are tarmacked and the rest are difficult and remote.

Obstacles come in all sizes and degrees, and the next one is simply the gate in a deer fence opening out onto the upper reaches of the Black Wood of Rannoch, where a few sparse spruce have eked out a living above the commercial treeline. The change in the character of the landscape from one side of the fence to the other is utterly flagrant. It's the exact type of transformation that's obvious when you cover country by bicycle. You're going quickly and smoothly enough not to be distracted by the details that can make walking such a pleasure. On a bike, there is an element of skimming over a landscape, which half disengages the mind while expanding the scale and scope of perception.

The change in atmosphere is palpable as I close the gate on the open, featureless grouse moor behind and enter what feels like the safety of the forest, even though the trees are stunted and scattered. I've come through the inhuman and returned to the human; land with a purpose I can share.

* * *

Setting off down into the wood, the track immediately degenerates. Here at the summit, where estate and forest meet, it seems as if the path may have recently been ploughed. It's certain that there is little traffic between the two worlds. The suspension components creak, groan and whistle as they soak up the ruts and stones, and these noises pique the interest of the forest birds, a few finches flitting across above me. They're the first birds I've seen since I left Innerwick in Glen Lyon, underlining the relative sterility of the pass behind me.

I've rarely felt any desire to look backwards so far and this is no exception. I turn my back on the bleak heather and my thoughts forward, matching what I can see through the binoculars to the north with what I see on the map. In the far distance I can clearly pick out the track I'll be climbing up from the far side of Loch Rannoch this afternoon, a winding beige scar across a khaki hillside defended by blocks of forest in Civil War formations; pike squares and lines of musketeers.

The Black Wood of Rannoch has a long history, not only as a royal forest that dates back to the early 1500s, but also as a remnant of the more or less mythical Caledonian forest. It now belongs to the Forestry Commission, established when Britain realised how ill-prepared it had been for the First World War. The whole country ran on coal and needed to replace vast imports of wood for pit props. In the aftermath, the Commission was set up to plant, grow and manage a strategic stock of timber for any future emergency. One duly arrived in the shape of the Second World War, and in light of the fundamental changes to society that it brought, the Commission evolved into a body that takes account of the beauty and recreational value of our forests as well as the strategic value. It now owns about one acre in ten of the country, and whilst its main aim remains timber production, it recognises that forests can be the wildlife reserves, wild gardens and places to play we all need simply to be human. Anyone who's been remotely interested in mountain biking in the last ten years will know about the 7Stanes network of trail centres established across the south of the country where access is free and the Commission makes its money from parking and renting space out to cafés and bike shops – just the kind of project that proves sport for us can easily live side by side with more traditional land use.

Although the trees are small and sparse at the top of the hill, dropping down the wide forest track soon brings me between walls of tall conifers and I lose sight of the opposite side of the loch and the Cairngorms beyond. One of the greatest and most under-rated advantages of travelling by bicycle is that you can smell the land as you cross it. In the top of the Rannoch woods the odour is quite delicious, a musty bisque of mushrooms and earth with a sharp, fresh top note from the conifers. If anyone ever makes an aftershave that smells like a pine forest in summer, I will be a very loyal client.

The pleasure of freewheeling through the shady, finely perfumed wood sees me picking up a little more speed than I'd thought, and before I know it there's a lochan on my left where none should be. A glance at the map alerts me to my first proper navigational error. It's nothing serious, just a warning to avoid dreaming in unfamiliar country. No harm could have come of it as all the forest roads lead down to the loch eventually, but I've picked a way down that follows a long, straight burn, the Allt na Bogair, on one side of what seems to be quite a deep gorge lined with mature trees, and I don't want to miss that.

I've spotted my mistake in good time and it's only a hundred metres back to the turn with, more importantly, maybe only ten metres of counter-climb. The track down the side of the burn isn't a Land Rover track, as I'd expected from the map, but the most perfect single-track, the delight of all real cross-country mountain bikers, undulating and gently swinging from side to side on dry, springy soil carpeted with pine needles. The roots of the mature pine trees make for just the right type of bump for my short-travel suspension to float over as I swing between their trunks, the trailer quite forgotten despite the rattling of its links. This is mountain cycling at its most perfect: hypnotic, effortless progress over idyllic scenery towards a tryst with my lady in a Highland refuge.

Although I'm immersed in the effort of keeping the bike on track, and revelling in the pure pleasure of having gravity on my side again, here in this ancient woodland there's something else besides the joy I'm feeling: an acute awareness that I need to remember how this feels. Some time in my life, if I'm lucky, I'll be old and frail and not able to ride a bike. Some time, maybe, they'll have me plumbed and wired into machines and nurses will smile sympathetically and call me by my first name, and I will need this memory of a journey to a higher, cooler place with the smell of resin and the sound of wild water on rock.

And then, something occurs that I'd almost given up hope on happening. Two recreational mountain bikers have chosen to cycle up this delectable track and we are closing fast. Their bikes are new, brightly coloured and clean, and their clothes are in expensive, muted tones of grey and brown. I can't imagine quite what they make of the cycle-tramp riding an ancient hybrid and a cheap trailer down the trail towards them, so I pull off the track to let them pass. This gives them the chance to chat if they want to, but they don't seem keen to engage beyond a simple greeting and continue to climb on up through the woods. They may just be horrified to see vegetable oil being used as chain lube. There is a snobbish element in all cycling disciplines, after all.

The thing with cycling downhill is that it never lasts long enough. For everyone but masochists it's the paradigm of what cycling should be: the odd turn of the cranks and the wind rushing past as you wing your way wherever you're headed. It never lasts and except for those of us willing to accept mechanical assistance it's always well and hard earned. For me, the rush comes to an end with a T-junction and the start of the family forest walks that signal a return to the gentler slopes and the realities of the world at road level. Crossing a wooden bridge gives a first and last look at the Allt na Bogair, which I could hear but never see all the way down through the forest.

A few minutes later, I drift past a young German family picnicking with immaculate manners in the car park. I wish them *bon appétit*, first because I haven't enough German to say it in that language, and second because English doesn't have a decent way to send this most basic of human messages. 'Enjoy your food' is something I might say sardonically to the cat as he sticks his snout in whatever reconstituted carrion it is they make cat food from, but it's not a way I could ever address strangers. Even here on the trail, food is so much more than fuel, and it's with a slight start that I realise I haven't had my own lunch yet. It's time to find out what the hamlet of Kinloch Rannoch has to offer.

Loch Rannoch is a dead-end in the road system because the western limit of the glen is the wide, desolate and quite intractable Rannoch Moor, a place where roads are dragged down into the bog by the goblins before they're even finished. There's barely a footpath across it, though the West Highland railway line I rode under at the Glen Auch viaduct does skirt its eastern edge. There's just no practical way for a road to link out west to Fort William and so there's no through traffic. As a result, the flat road that loops the loch is quiet enough to be used both by time trial riders and families having a day out. I won't be catching the racers with my chunky tyres, luggage and tired legs but the five kilometres through the wooded lochside to the village of Kinloch Rannoch shouldn't take long, though on the way I'm flagged down by the driver of a Hydro Board four-by-four looking for his colleagues. I haven't seen them but it's a nice vignette of Highland life; the human touch needed in an area with little phone reception.

After a few short minutes of luxuriously smooth tarmac I'm wrestling the bike into a position where it will stay put against the wall of the village store. Judging by the exterior, the journey inside, although only a few steps, will mean going back two or three decades. It's a very welcome part of the Highland retail experience that brings back memories of childhood summer holidays with unknown local brands of fizzy pop sold in shops that would also supply a fishing permit and a paraffin lamp. True to form, the shop has that sleepy *mañana* feel and a timeless range of goods best described as post-war without being too specific about which one. Things like tinned potatoes. I've never known anyone that would admit to eating tinned potatoes but there must be a ghillie or a stalker living in a remote cottage on the moor somewhere who comes in twice a year and clears out the shelves.

Such delights are not for me as I've a reasonably eccentric shopping list of my own to take care of. First off, I need oil. Everyone needs oil some time and as there isn't another shop for twenty miles they will have it, next to the lightbulbs and the fly spray. It's 3-in-1, which is as good as I can hope for, but it's seen as no more than a lightweight stopgap in the cycling world. Bike lubricants generally come in a variety of weights appropriate to riding in California, Europe or here in the Highlands, where oil any thinner than golden syrup will wash off before the day's out, something I know full well but failed to plan for. But 3-in-1 is better than vegetable oil and I've now got a whole can of the stuff, so that can be crossed off the list.

Next item: a bottle of wine for tonight, if you don't mind. Preferably the finest available to humanity but if it's red, not actually sweet and contains alcohol, it will go fine with my risotto. Given that I'm not so bursting with energy that I want to lug a glass bottle over the Cairngorms for no reason, I'll need a plastic bottle into which to decant whatever magnificent vintage I can secure. I pissed into the previous one at four o'clock this morning, and I could put it through a dishwasher but drinking out of it would still be repulsive. Tonic water sounds like a refreshing way of washing my lunch down and the bottle will do fine provided I don't somehow end up with tonic wine, a concoction known to be dangerous in these parts. The sandwiches look faded but I'm beyond gastronomy so I grab a handful and, realising that I'm actually physically craving salt, a packet of crisps to go with them. Faded sandwiches, crisps and tonic water: the lunchtime feast of adventure riders the globe over, I believe. It's time to find a bench and sit down properly. I've come to appreciate that seats are precious and much under-rated things.

There's a bench right outside the shop and I park myself with real relief to bask in the fair weather and see what's happening in the streets of the town. The main thing is that all the household rubbish bins are locked and the tourists can't find anywhere to put their ice cream wrappers. A family comes past on the pavement, all of them either pushing or riding impeccably clean bikes, which I guess they've just hired and I hope they can find somewhere safe to ride. When I was a loon, bikes were for getting away from your folks, tearing round the lanes and pavements. It doesn't seem to be too fashionable now with the middle classes to let your kids ride off on their own, and while I suppose it must be good to share a bike ride with your kids, the great thing about bicycles is that learning to ride one cuts you loose from pedestrian constraints at a stroke. There's room for organised races and rides in any cyclist's life but I hope these children grow up to be adventurers plotting their own ways.

Although I've offered eye contact and a smile to everyone who's passed, no one has stopped to talk. I'm grubby and I don't doubt that I smell like a dog's basket so that's not a surprise, but as I get wired into my sandwiches I notice that a gentleman in early middle age has returned my smile, nervously but with definite curiosity. He's dressed in a threadbare suit, a white shirt stretched fairly tight over his belly and a tartan knitted tie. There's a plastic shopping bag in his hand and I immediately like him and feel a bit protective towards him. He walks past once and after a few minutes comes back, scoping out the new boy in town. On the second pass, I nod to him and he hesitates, looking at the trailer with its Lion Rampant flag.

'Are you in favour of the royal family?' he asks, in a way that's amicable but oddly formal, drawing himself up straight as he says it.

'Not really, no,' I reply.

'That is their flag,' he asserts. 'You can't use it.'

'Ah, yes,' I agree. 'That's why I chose it. Five years in prison, I believe, if the Lord Lyon finds out you've been flying it, ten if he catches you in Glen Lyon. Are you in favour of the royal family yourself?'

It's a strange opening to a conversation; direct but perfectly friendly. We talk a bit about the politics of the land and who we are. He fell off a bus when he was a child, hurt his head quite badly and has never really worked – the kind of man who'd be best looked after by a village like this where everyone can keep an eye out for him. I hope they do, anyway.

When I ask what he does to keep himself busy, the answer is so unexpected that for a brief moment I think he might be making fun of me.

'Trainspotting.'

He can't know that I bid for the contract to translate that famous book into French a long time ago, can he? Surely not, but we're thirty kilometres from the West Highland line at Rannoch Station and twenty from the Perth to Inverness line at Pitlochry. Then again, there must be locals driving up and down to both of those places all the time and he can maybe get a lift easily enough. He seems serious.

When he asks where I'm headed, I don't know why but I answer something vague about taking the pass through to Loch Garry, but of course he knows all the places round here and immediately proposes that I'm heading to one of the Gaelic villages, Duinish or Saunich. He thinks these remote spots held out as linguistic bastions against the Anglophone incursion up the glen, perhaps not in our lifetimes but in the lifetimes of people he knew; maybe his grandparents. He tells me there was a cheese press still at Duinish until recently but that it might have been removed to become a garden ornament by someone who may or may not have had the right to do that. It has the sound of the kind of colourful local tale that gets embroidered as it's handed from generation to generation and I don't really want to get into too much of the detail of it so I take my leave. We shake hands as he wishes me well for the rest of the trip.

* * *

Back on the tarmac and heading west round the north shore of the loch, the road passes right under the walls of the Loch Rannoch Highland Club, which may well be the source of the cycling families in the village. A hardcore path, laid so that the residents don't need to mix with the cars to reach the village, runs beside the road. In the middle of this vast landscape, with the magnificent view of the conical mountain Schiehallion behind me, and Loch Rannoch itself stretching to the horizon, it's impossible not to be struck by the density of the units of the country club, stacked up and almost spilling out onto the road. I can understand why people come here; it's beautiful. But in Canada or Sweden a loch of this size would be ringed with small houses and wooden huts for weekends and holidays. Here, Loch Rannoch's forty kilometres of shoreline are owned by six estates and the Forestry Commission, and I guess they're not for selling to the common man. If you want to spend the night round here, you're crammed into the village or the resort if you're not willing to sling a tent in the woods.

There are two ways in from the side of Loch Rannoch to Duinish: one from Annat and one from Aulich. The Annat one is slightly shorter but I know it's quite rough and the better made track in from Aulich is calling out to my tired legs. Another attraction is that I want to use the oldest roads that I can and this one is an ancient drove road, marked on the 1755 Roy map.

Ambling past the entrance to the Annat track, I'm intrigued by the oddly named Chemical Cottages. They're on the site of what was marked on the 1873 Ordnance Survey map as the Northern Chemical Works, a name to pique the interest of any chemist. Given the date and location I can't think of many things they could have been doing other than distilling wood for pyroligneous acid, a kind of rough industrial vinegar. There is no trace of the works now other than the name of these cottages. Maybe their name in turn will pass into legend like the nearby Clach a' Mharsainte, the Stone of the Merchant, where the name of the merchant in question, throttled against the rock by the straps of his own loaded pack, is long lost.

Moving on westward up the tarmac B-road, I pass the entrance to the lodge that belongs to the owner of the land I'll be crossing and sleeping on tonight. One of those charming signs asks us all to respect the privacy of the owner, which shouldn't be too difficult given that the land belongs to a company in the Channel Island of Jersey. We are entering into the mysterious world of Astel Ltd, registered purpose: 'The management and exploitation of woodlands.'

A little further on the old road up, the Aulich Burn appears beside a cluster of caravans, which are most likely temporary accommodation for workers on the estate. I turn in and clamber down into the cool, damp and shady course of the burn to fill my water bottle before starting the final climb of the day, another two hundred and fifty metres' ascent to the bothy on the watershed between this loch and Loch Garry.

The track is smooth, new and packed hard by the passage of construction vehicles. It turns and twists through a birch wood where, to my delight, I notice the first chanterelles of the year, the egg-yolk yellow caps of the mushrooms dotted about the stony trackside and the short grass under the trees. Their appearance is as magical as it is ironic given that I'm packing a supermarket freeze-dried mushroom risotto for my evening meal. I am sorely tempted to stop and gather a few perfect specimens to add to my dinner but something holds me back – not the scutter of frying them on a stove in a bothy but just some kind of clash of mentalities. I'm on a mission, climbing up out of one glen to a watershed. I have a rendezvous and this is no time to be pottering about in a wood gathering mushrooms. The notion is quite absurd, of course: this is the perfect time to gather mushrooms. They're fresher than you'd ever get them from a fancy Italian grocer, they're free and they're practically crying out to be added to tonight's meal. But no, I take nothing but the pleasure of knowing they're there and keep grinding on up the track, popping out of the birch wood and into the bleak khaki wasteland that I saw in the far distance from the top of Rannoch wood about noon.

It's heather moorland, as sweeping and bare as only heather moorland can be. The freshly remade track only serves to under-line this bleakness, as do the disconsolate squeakings of the meadow pipits, the only wildlife round here. The heather and the bleakness are, presumably, a choice, not an accident or an obliga-tion. On estates such as this, deer have no one hunting them but us, sheep are counted out and in, and most muir-burning is done to a plan drawn up by a human being. This landscape is maintained by whoever controls Astel Ltd. It must suit them for some reason, but I don't believe it can be for the beauty of the thing. The birch wood down by the lodge, with the silver verticals of the trunks set against the emerald grass dotted with orange mushrooms, is beau-tiful. But this is blasted and empty to the point of being unsettling.

It's been a deer forest since 1887 and the upland farming subsi-dies paid for keeping land free of scrub and trees, combined with management for shooting, probably explain its grim condition. But no one has any duty to stand up in public and say why they keep birches round their home while other parts of the estate have just a skinny layer of heather and a few gloomy Sitka spruce woods. We are allowed to access our land, but we may not nec-essarily know *why* it is the way it is, or even who decides how it is. My progress is fast over the hard-packed surface and there is little here to slow down for other than the grand sweep and roll of the hills, though it's like seeing a fine set of cheekbones with the skin stripped off.

As I approach the watershed, there's a grinding noise and a sullen resistance to further rotation of the cranks transmitted up through the wheels, chain and pedals. Clearly something is gravely, and potentially fatally, wrong with some part of the rig. No warning, no hint of trouble, just a near-instantaneous transformation of my self-contained and self-propelled land cruising machine into an immobile heap of metal pipes, bars and rods. Turning round, it's all too obvious exactly what the problem is: the trailer has snapped in two and ploughed a neat furrow in the gravel. The kingpin, a steel rod twenty centimetres long running vertically through the main pivot between the body of the trailer and the forks that attach it to the rear axle of the bike, has snapped. It both bears the weight of the front of the trailer and allows it to turn to follow the line of the bike in corners. It is quite vital to the entire undertaking and I do not have a spare one with me.

This immediate and purely mechanical and logistical problem jolts me out of the gloom that had settled on me whilst thinking about the landscape. Clear and realistic thinking is needed if the journey isn't to end here with a humiliating walk back to Kinloch Rannoch. I'm startled by my own reaction to this unwelcome development. There is no emotion at all, not anger at the broken piece, or at myself for not noticing or for buying a cheap trailer in the first place. There's no sadness at the prospect of abandoning a trip after years of planning and three days of hard cycling. There's no amusement, either, though I would look pretty ridiculous to a dispassionate observer.

In place of emotion a plan immediately forms in my mind, based on the simple facts of biology, geography and physics. The first part is very simple – not to get cold or upset, and that just means putting on a few layers from my rucksack to avoid a chill setting in after I've sweated my way up to this exposed place. Secondly, get the map out and figure out exactly where I am between the road and the bothy, to see how long it will take me to walk or cycle to either. There's nothing wrong with the bike itself so I can easily ride onwards or back, though it means abandoning the bulk of my kit. There's no mobile signal here at all, so whatever I do has to take into account the fact that Nathalie will be waiting for me at the bothy five kilometres further on. That means that the best alternative to fixing the trailer here – if that can be done – is to ride on with my sleeping bag and rations for tonight to meet her and then see how the land lies tomorrow.

With that plan comes the comfort of knowing that this voyage isn't over just yet. I can allow myself to unhitch the trailer and have a look at the contents of both the waterproof bag and my rucksack to see if there's any way to cobble this thing back together. The kingpin is shattered, one end broken off and now lost somewhere on the trail, and unlikely to be any use. As any adventurer must, I have a good range of cable ties with which you can certainly fix many things, but the combined roles of load-bearing and pivot make this a demanding job.

I know that there's a wire frame inside my rucksack as I have a vivid memory of the embarrassment of getting hauled out of line in airport security because of it. It's a bit weedy for the job, but it could possibly be pressed into use here. I don't really want to pull my rucksack apart, and I can't imagine the wire being strong enough to take the pounding that crossing the Gaick will give it, but it is an option.

And then it strikes me. The flag on the trailer is mounted on a fibreglass pole. Surely it won't fit in the axis of the pivot? I offer the rod up to the bearing body ... and it slips in. A perfect fit. So far, despite the solitude, I haven't been talking to myself much at all, but this time it's justified and I allow myself a 'No…' tinged with wonder at the magic of the situation. I've rescued a trip from one side of the country to the other by literally planting the Royal Standard in the middle of the problem. I appear to be living some kind of patriotic allegory. The elegance of the solution just spurs me to get going even quicker. With a couple of cable ties secured as tight as possible to delay the pole's inevitable journey up and out of its berth or down into the ground, the newly bodged contraption is loaded up and ready to go.

In the space of fifteen minutes I've gone from a potentially terminal equipment failure to being back on the road with a lash-up every bit as elegant as it is absurd. By adventure I've got myself into a sticky situation, and by invention and the suppression of emotion I've got myself out of that same trouble. I haven't sought or asked for help, even though it must be at hand somewhere. It always is if you tell people you're in trouble. I don't know why but it feels to me as I'm standing here that the person who controls this estate is of a hard and practical bent. This landscape seems like the product of a general and specific suppression of emotions, of empathy with the natural world. It's a hard, cold place shorn of ornament, stripped of anywhere to retreat or hide.

The first few turns of the pedals are as cautious as they must be. I'm acutely aware that every bump in the track is now causing the two separate parts of the trailer to bite into the fibreglass rod like a pair of scissors. The rod's surface is nowhere near as hard as steel and it will be cut through eventually, the only question being just when. How far can I go? And have the two cable ties got enough purchase on the surface of the rod to prevent it working out of its sleeve? Only time and distance will tell, and whatever happens the trailer pivot is going to be a nagging worry until I reach Findhorn or find a better solution.

Coaxing the bike and its load over the remaining handful of kilometres to the bothy reveals what I'd suspected to be the reason for the width and high quality of the track. A notice announces the construction of two small hydroelectric generation stations with a combined output of under a megawatt. We all need electricity and these things can be built into the land with great discretion but what ought to make us self-sufficient in energy may well profit 'Mr Astel' as landlord more than it does us as citizens and end-users. The Gaels of Duinish, long gone now, would surely wonder at the wealth tumbling out of the hills around their village, and I have to admire the boldness of the first man who declared that he owned Beinn Mholach – and there must have been such a man – before the bounty migrated into the hands of a mysterious corporate entity.

Cresting the last rise reveals a broad plain and, on the far side of it, under the camouflage slope of Meall Doire, the bothy. The track winds, but it's pretty flat and with a carefully picked-out route it's only a few minutes before I'm running the bike over the venerable stone slab bridge on the burn in front of the remains of an ancient hamlet. Right beside that bridge there's an upright stone planted in the turf, but it's not a handrail or anything else so workaday. The bowling pin shape gives it away: it's Bodach again. It looks like I'll be spending another night in his protection.

* * *

The bothy is a single-storey stone-built house with a ramshackle wooden porch that stands tucked into in a green hollow between two drumlins. The heathery one to the west, behind the bothy, looms high above the roof and must give decent shelter from the prevailing weather rattling in from the Atlantic. In front, there's a classic cute egg-shaped grassy mound, which blocks the direct view out across the braided burns and marshes of the confused bog on the watershed plain. Between the two, there's a magical space like the hollow of a cupped green hand, with the refuge cradled in the palm. The hills round about the flattish area of the watershed are whalebacks, coloured like the Airfix model bombers of my boyhood, in swirling patterns of olive, grey and brown where the heather has been burnt and grown back over the seasons. There is not one tree to be seen, lending the whole an air of almost industrial desolation.

When I was young, bothies were an almost mystical part of the hillwalking scene. Learning the locations of these open shelters was a rite of passage. You had to know someone who knew where they were, or just stumble on them in the hills. Although the internet has pretty much done away with the secrecy, it has done little to alter the fundamental charm or the uniqueness of the unwritten social contract that allows them to exist. The original purposes of the various bothies are mixed, but many are abandoned crofts or deer-watching stations established during the poaching boom around the turn of the last century. Now they're mostly owned by the shooting estates that cover the bulk of the Highlands and maintained either by the estates themselves or by volunteer groups, often at considerable expense and effort. The work goes into buildings that no one pays to use at all. Even using a bothy for a trip with a paid guide causes the bothy's owner to be liable for business rates, despite them not receiving a penny, and is strongly frowned upon, as is any other deviation from a strict code of etiquette.

The rules are pretty much that you only use a bothy for a couple of nights at a time, you rub along with anyone else staying there, and you leave the bothy and its surrounding land cleaner and tidier than you found them. There's no one to enforce these rules, no caretakers or attendants, but remarkably they are more or less obeyed. Some bothies have burnt down, and some people have left and pitched their tent for the night rather than share with a difficult occupant, but by and large the system works. The bothies themselves range from sheep-sheds to proper houses and are found anywhere from the roadside to the wildest and most remote spots in the kingdom. But we just manage to share them in a great web of anonymous communitarianism, all under the umbrella of a phalanx of sporting estates whose motivations for keeping the bothies open I can only guess at. It may be a desire for their wilderness to be shared by ordinary people; it may be a sense of *noblesse oblige*. Whatever it is, it just works. As a result, we have a totally unplanned and unmanned network of mountain shelters, some of which are quite eccentric, something not present in any other European country.

The bothy itself is a joy. I've been before and I know what to expect. The porch has a simple wooden gate to keep the sheep out, and in witness of that function it's festooned with wool. Behind it, the porch smells like the gate might not always have been fastened. It contains a selection of saws, an axe and a spade, along with a few bits of timber that have been put out of the rain to dry. The double front door swings aside as I knock and call out, just in case I'm intruding on anyone.

Inside, there's a roughly flagged room with a tall dresser and a fireplace that looks to have a bird nesting in the chimney above. To the left, a door gives on to an abandoned room in ruin and to the right another door leads into a wood-floored and panelled sanctuary. It's dry and it smells good – of nothing but the fire – and it has been immaculately swept and tidied by the last person to use it. There's a good wooden bench and a chair, but the summit of comfort is the two metal-framed vinyl-upholstered armchairs that seem to have escaped the attentions of the rodents that are numerous around any bothy. They can be drawn up to the fireplace for the evening and a smile spreads across my face at the thought of dinner with Nathalie and a glass of wine in the rustic comfort of a bleak and forgotten corner of Perthshire.

There's a fireplace but there won't be any fire unless I get some more wood. The restored part of the bothy isn't the whole of the building, as it looks like it might at one time have been a row of cottages. The north end of the bothy is now tumbling down and the beams and rafters are sitting on the grass where the floor used to be. I can't see any harm in harvesting them for the fire as they're just going to rot away otherwise. I drag what would once have been a section of an A-frame roof to the porch and set about it with the tools. The back of the axe makes a great hammer to get the two pieces apart, but the saws are all blunt. It's only half past five so I've loads of time to kill before Nathalie gets here and I set myself to the sawing, a slow process that only reveals how much stronger my legs are than my arms. It feels good and natural to be cutting wood to keep warm tonight, even if there isn't a tree for miles and I'm actually cannibalising the collapsed part of the house.

Although it's high summer, this is the north and we're four hundred metres above, and far from, the sea. It's not always warm of a summer evening round here. The physical heat from the fire is going to be very welcome, but of course the real reason I'm doing this is for the atmosphere and the emotional heat, to make Nathalie's arrival as warm and welcoming as it can be. As the sun goes down, the light will fade and the timber-lined room will be lit by the orange flicker from the grate. If that doesn't make for a romantic evening then I really am no judge of romance.

With the cosy evening fire going I can turn my mind to the

more prosaic matter of my socks. They've never really dried out since I hacked my way out of Glen Kinglass through the bogs and peat hags two days ago. In my experience, every bothy has a clothes line; it's the one thing that costs nothing and which every single visitor is likely to need. This one is right next to the fire and, after I've peeled off the offending items, I hang them as close to the warmth as I dare. Even I can smell the result, which isn't nearly as bad as it could be and should dissipate before it wrecks the intimate ambiance I'm aiming for. The simple pleasure of having fresh socks on is luxurious and I'm keen to have dry feet tomorrow. I reckon I can get the socks dry and put away in an hour or so. If I do that then I can just deny all knowledge of any musty smells. I lay out my sleeping bag on the bench, and my cooking kit for the evening on the table by the window, and step outside to take the air.

The drumlin in front of the bothy gives the perfect vantage point to get early sight of Nathalie coming in from the north, and the dry, springy turf makes for a comfortable seat where I can just let the scale of the place swim over me – from the Allt Shallainn tumbling down to the east, to the tall hills flanking the unseen Loch Garry to the north, and the broad, wild marsh to the west. The solitude of my days on the trail means that I'm not expecting anyone to come after me from the south, but from my perch I spot movement on the track I've just come up. Turning the binoculars that way reveals a black four-by-four, which at this time of day I can only guess belongs to the estate rather than the engineers on the hydroelectric scheme. I track it in and out of the dips in the road and drop the binoculars when it's close enough for the occupants to see me. Whoever they are, I don't want to seem too curious.

After a few minutes the vehicle reaches the turn-off to the bothy and turns in, gently crosses the stone slab bridge and comes to a halt. Before the 2003 Act came into force I'd been chased off moorland by gamekeepers and I'm half expecting the standard 'Can we just ask who you are and what you're doing here?' enquiry, which is the very modern and very gentle version of 'Get off my land'. What happens next is so unexpected that I actually rock backwards a bit. Three ladies descend from the vehicle; two younger, one older, but all of them dressed in top-of-the-range knitwear in beautiful muted colours and vaguely bohemian style. If this is the welcome party dispatched by the estate to see me off their domain then it's clearly an estate like no other. Both my manners and my inquisitiveness mean that there is no way I can stay sat on top of my drumlin while these elegant ladies mill about a wilderness refuge below me, so I stretch, stand up and make my way down the slope to greet them.

Some instinct has me offer my hand to shake. Despite the wild setting (or perhaps because of it), a formal greeting feels proper and dignified, acting to reduce any tension between us. I don't suppose they were expecting to find anyone here, but they seem completely unfazed by the slightly peculiar situation, despite the fact that they are speaking with an angular and dishevelled stranger dressed in black and smelling like anyone would after a couple of days' cycling through the hills. I tell them my name and my business before they get a chance to ask. They don't reciprocate with any story of their own, but that doesn't seem odd at all.

'Do you think we could take a look around inside the bothy?' asks the lady who was at the wheel of the vehicle. I can't place her accent, but it isn't from around these parts.

'Of course,' I reply. 'Bothies are open to anyone, but I do have to apologise in advance. I'm afraid I'm drying my socks in front of the fire.'

'Oh, don't worry about that!' is the confident, cheerful reply and the three of them head off into the bothy for a nose around.

I can't remember if there was a gate at the entrance to the estate track; it certainly wasn't locked if there was one, so these ladies could be anyone from anywhere. They could be tourists following a satnav, for all I know, though their vehicle isn't brand new by any stretch. They are very pleasant and self-assured, maybe locals of some kind.

I retreat back up my perch to continue scanning the horizon for any sign of Nathalie. She's a mountaineer and hillwalker so I've no real concerns, but I know that the last kilometre or two of the approach from the north is trackless and requires a small river crossing. On top of that, the bothy's tucked out of sight until the last moment, so there is a slight worry that won't go away until I see her strolling down the heathery bank.

From my vantage point I can hear the ladies' voices when they spill back out into the cool summer evening. I can recognise quite a few European languages but I can't at all place their language, not even roughly, and this new element of mystery piques my interest enough to have me strolling down again to meet them at their car.

'I hope my socks didn't overwhelm you,' I offer, apologetically.

'No, of course not.' They laugh.

'I don't wish to pry, but I'd be fascinated to know which language you were speaking amongst yourselves just now. I didn't recognise it at all.'

'Well, you wouldn't,' laughs the leader of the group. 'It's Latvian. No one speaks Latvian but Latvians.'

This answer has me intrigued beyond reason and I tell them so, apparently to their amusement.

'May I be so bold as to ask what brings three Latvian ladies to one of the most remote dwellings in Perthshire?' I ask. The question seems to send a slight flicker of embarrassment across the driver's face, but not enough for me to regret asking.

'Well, it's mine,' she says, turning to the bothy.

'The bothy's yours?' I ask in surprise.

'The bothy, yes, and all of this,' she replies, indicating the surrounding hills with a serene but slightly bashful look.

The answer makes my head birl. I know perfectly well who owns the bothy and the hills around and it's Astel Ltd of St. Helier, Jersey. As social situations go, it's wildly exciting and slightly uncomfortable. Given that I'm planning to spend the night in wood-panelled comfort, I can hardly confront the lady claiming to be my host with any suggestion that she isn't the owner. And I don't doubt her for a moment. Her poise of a few minutes ago makes perfect sense now. I don't think I've met a landowner on their own turf before, apart from a warmly remembered childhood encounter with Lord Thurso. There is no way I can help myself trying to tease out a little more information.

'May I ask how you came to own the estate?' I ask. 'What would draw you to this place so strongly that you would buy it?'

'Well, it's my husband that owns it,' she replies. 'He's British ... well, English.' The correction is telling. It may be that locals have made the distinction clear in the past.

It feels wrong to pry about the husband, but I am keen to know what a Latvian makes of this terrain.

'Well, we have quite similar weather, but we have trees on our land,' is the answer. She may or may not know that the absence of trees here is quite deliberate, a consequence of the area having been a deer forest and grouse moor since Victorian times. She's very warm and open and seems to have no sense of entitlement whatsoever. It's quite disorientating and I love the fact that she asked permission to go inside her own house, no matter how rudimentary. That showed real class.

We get to chatting about my own journey and what's brought me here. Their charm is undeniable, and the drop of their jaws when I tell them where I set off from is perfectly judged, indicating neither dismissiveness nor adulation. They're really interested in how I can transport all my food and camping gear and I show them the trailer, which is empty now that all my stuff is laid out in the bothy.

The oldest of the three, who has turned out to be the mother of the driver and the other lady, is hugely amused and, knowing that I'm expecting Nathalie to join me shortly, gleefully asks if I'm going to carry her standing up in the trailer like it was a chariot and she was my Queen. The image is absurd enough to have us all laughing and any barriers there may have been melt away. We get to talking about the bothy, and the lady I now know to be the owner declares that not only does she love it, she wants as many people to use it as possible so that they can get the same joy from the landscape as she does. That's an idea at once so natural and human, but at the same time so far from my expectations for the owner of a shooting estate, that again I'm at a slight loss. It's like conversational judo and has me countering that she might not want to make the bothy too comfortable if she doesn't want to attract the wrong crowd.

She actually asks what she could do to make the bothy better and I suggest that if she's got money to spend then solar-powered lighting for the evenings would be brilliant. Most bothies have a range of candles, lamps and wind-up torches lying around, and a solar lighting system with batteries would be a boon for hikers, especially outside the summer season. The other thing lacking is fast-flowing water of the kind I'd be confident drinking, so I suggest that if there's any spare pipes left after the installation of the hydroelectric station, maybe she could run a line down from the river to the bothy. I almost suggest getting the contractors to dump their waste wood here as firewood, but hold back, knowing that the availability of firewood is exactly what attracts the crazy element.

'What are you eating tonight?' the owner asks out of nowhere.

'Oh well, I've saved myself a freeze-dried mushroom risotto as a treat,' I reply as humbly as I can.

'Which way did you come in?' she asks. 'Was it from Rannoch?' I confirm that it was, intrigued.

'Did you come up through the birch wood?'

'I did.'

'Did you see the chanterelles?'

'I did, yes...'

'Well, we've a pork roast cooking back at the house with chanterelles. Would you like us to go and get you some? You could heat it on your stove.'

'That is one of the most generous offers anyone has ever made to me.'

It puts me in mind of General Wade's indignant report that the Highlanders 'are treated by their Chiefs with great Familiarity, they partake with them in their Diversions, and shake them by the hand wherever they meet them'.

'But I couldn't possibly accept. That's a twelve-mile round trip, I couldn't possibly put you to the bother. I have my rations, I'll be fine.'

The disappointment on the owner's face is real, and I'm slightly ashamed at not accepting her offer. She clearly regards me now as her guest, but there's a stubborn grain in me that insists on preserving my status as an independent traveller. I may have had a sandwich out of the Kinloch Rannoch store for lunch, but there's something about accepting this wildly generous offer – not just to share their dinner but to transport it to me in a four-by-four – that just doesn't feel right. I adore pork with chanterelles. I've made it many times myself with mushrooms gathered fresh from a very similar wood. The hospitality that's being proposed is utterly seductive and I know that Nathalie would be overjoyed to find a pot of home cooking on the go when she gets here. She'd be tickled pink, in fact. And yet…

It's more complicated than just not wanting to put strangers to an extravagant level of bother on my account. It's deviating from my logistical plan that bothers me. My risotto is a treat to mark the middle of five nights on the road, and I've been working through my stack of food in the way you might watch the fuel gauge of a car.

And there's another layer on top of that. Accepting the roast would breach my unspoken ideal of making the trip with the resources I carry and what I can glean from the villages I pass through. I know that what I'm doing here is acting out a charade of autonomy, a kind of personal North British *Juche*, the North Korean philosophy of total self-reliance. No human being is entirely reliant on their own efforts, no matter how heroic. The reality is that we come into the world at the hands of a team and most of us will leave it the same way. I may have assembled the bits of the bike I'm riding but I didn't make them and I didn't mine the ore for the steel and alloy. I didn't grow the beans in my breakfast packs and there is something more than a little petulant in turning down what is a gracious and extraordinary offer that almost breaches the fourth wall of the theatre of power between lodge and bothy. But my obstinate pride won't have it. Freeze-dried space food will be just fine for the rocket man.

As a last effort to breach my defences, the owner lady, no doubt taking account of my ideas about the water supply here, proposes to give me a couple of litres of mineral water from the vehicle. Already feeling shame at my inability to give in gracefully, I manage to accept this simplest token of shared humanity.

The four-by-four makes its way back out across the stone slab bridge and off south to dinner and comfortable beds in the lodge. I really liked all of them, friendly, open and generous as they were, but I wouldn't go with them for anything. The wild tranquillity of this dell with its half-ruined bothy creeps back from behind the bluff, and my eyes turn once more to the north and the expectation of Nathalie's arrival. The sun is now flirting with the summits of the Talla Beith forest to the north-west and I wonder if everything's all right. But the concern doesn't last long as, to my great surprise, the *bleu, blanc, rouge* of her bicycle appears down the track. I'd expected her to walk in, but here she is, grinning from ear to ear with simple pleasure as she cuts the corner and bounces down onto the turf in front of the bothy.

There's a flurry of hugs and bags and stories as I usher her inside to see our nest for the night. It's late enough that we're sure to have the place to ourselves and I think the evening is going to be convivial and cosy, an expectation that's only deepened as Nathalie gets a bottle of wine and two cans of beer from her bag. For some absurd reason, entirely in keeping with the moment, the cans bear the likeness of French football legend Eric Cantona. There is also a bottle of chain lube and a pair of brake blocks to make sure the bike doesn't feel left out.

There's a rule in bothies that you use any firewood sparingly, as it's almost always scarce. All the same I've a slightly heavy hand with the timber as the sun goes down and the room is filled with the orange glow of the flames and the smell of wood smoke. We both draw our leatherette armchairs as close to the grate as we can and just let our minds wander, hypnotised by the pulsing radiance of the embers. I don't know if the risotto has chanterelles in it, but it is very good, topped with fresh cheese and swilled with red wine from a tin mug. It is striking how content you can feel without so much as a bed to sleep in.

Four

Atholl

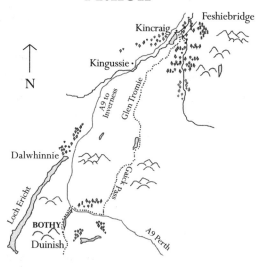

The night's sleep was deep and restful, apart from getting up once to blunder outside for a pee in the pitch black – a trip that was no longer than strictly necessary due to the inevitable ambush by famished midges. In the morning the absolute silence makes for a peaceful doze, even on the wooden floor, until the sun streaming in the window fully wakens me.

Getting coffee and beans ready is becoming increasingly reflex, and I look forward to breakfast, but I'm still unsure about the Gaick Pass. It's the highest point of the ride and will see me leaving Tayside for Speyside. There is no doubt that it's remote country and the map shows at least three river crossings, but there's nothing in all that to justify the anxiety I feel. The last few days haven't lacked in altitude, wildness or rivers, and I've been fine. And now I have brake blocks to change, a chain to clean and oil, and a trailer

116

to mend – enough to distract me from my worries. The first two take barely any effort at all, but the trailer is a poser. The flagpole solution has a certain simple beauty about it, but I just can't see it lasting. I've no sense of how resistant to the constant rubbing fibreglass is and I want to have a fall-back option with me if it should break later on today.

The bothy is palatially appointed compared to the one in Glen Kinglass, but it doesn't contain all that much that could reasonably be cannibalised. There are pots and cutlery in the cupboard in the antechamber but I now know who they belong to and I won't touch them. When you're looking for something but you don't know what, you have to look at the world in a different way from how you do when you've lost a specific thing. You need to turn off your seeking mind and open wide to possibilities, scanning not just the places where people put things, but floors, roofs, outhouses and holes. After a few minutes of this open-minded questing, I spot a coil of thick fencing wire on top of the dresser containing the crockery. It's soft iron but thick, at about five millimetres, and not easy to bend by hand. I beat it straight using the back of the axe and set about it with the cutting blades of my pliers, working them back and forward until the metal gives way. I now have a piece about twenty centimetres longer than the broken kingpin, enough to fold down a piece top and bottom to secure it in the pivot hole. I know this kind of wire well and I reckon it will make a decent replacement, but as much for my amusement as anything I'm willing to stick with the flag for the moment, so I stow the wire in the bottom of the trailer bag as an emergency measure.

After the now routine wander away from the bothy with my toilet bag and trenching tool for the most discreet of natural needs, it's time to set the bothy in order and mount up. All of our rubbish has to be bagged, the hearth swept and the ashes dispersed. The bothy's guest book needs filling in with a brief account of who we are and what we're up to, and the floor swept, the tools stowed and the three-in-one oil left in the tin box for any future traveller with a rusty chain. I've no doubt there will be one. I make a mental note to bring a whetstone for the axe in the porch the next time I pass. It's so blunt it's more like a pointy hammer than a cutting tool.

The days are long and we're in no particular hurry. The hydro-electric construction workers start to arrive as I'm loading and hitching the trailer in front of the porch. They're clearly on the lookout for anyone in the bothy and wave as they pass. I guess they're in the caravans I passed, or maybe bed and breakfasts in Kinloch Rannoch. I can certainly think of less attractive commutes to work, though this must be a bleak place in winter.

Closing the front door behind us, I know that we'll be back some time. The glow of the previous night is still in me and, although it's perched on a watershed amongst hills that aren't on any list of classics, this refuge in its green hollow is a welcoming place. With that thought, the reality sets in. I need to get to the other side of the Cairngorms today and that's not a trivial undertaking, no matter which way you go. These hills have been a serious barrier to travel for centuries and are as remote and wild as any in our country. But the process is the same as cycling through town to work. Sling your leg over the bike, turn the cranks and keep turning them until you get there.

Crossing the Allt Shallainn by the old timber bridge brings us into a construction site, all plywood and tyre tracks and stacks of pipes in timber braces. The noise of vehicles is inescapable and the track churned up to the point of being impassable. We stop to chat to a couple of workmen, just to get a sense of who they are, which turns out to be contractors from Falkirk, travelling up and down each week. They're hoping to get finished before the first snows, a wish I can wholeheartedly understand.

As soon as we're clear of the building site, we're dumped out into the only couple of kilometres of the route with no track marked on my OS map. As suits any watershed worthy of the name, it's a flattish area of braided burns, quagmires, saturated turf and heather. It's obvious in places that quad bikes or maybe a Land Rover pass here from time to time, but there's no real use in trying to ride the bikes for more than a few metres just to make the point that it is possible. A few of the burns have planks laid across them and it's fun to try to keep the bike and trailer on one plank while I walk the other. There's no prospect of getting lost as the weather is good and the hills either side of Loch Garry point the way towards the distant wall of the Cairngorms, so it's just a question of looking for the least saturated ground available in the next five or six metres and then repeating that process until we're out of the bog.

The river, when we get there, is low enough to ford by stepping on the tops of exposed boulders and pushing the bike and trailer alongside. Bicycle bearings don't much appreciate being underwater but there's no way of avoiding it on this trip. The whole bike will be stripped, cleaned and re-greased afterwards, if it survives, and the trailer may well be heading for the skip. It just needs to last another three days and my ears are becoming finely tuned to its every squeak and groan as it lunges into dips and grates its wire mesh belly over stones. I'm going to be the poor thing's nursemaid until we hit the North Sea. My folly in penny-pinching on the trailer, while lavishing the bicycle with decent components, has been starkly exposed. The weak link has broken, just as anyone else would have predicted. I'd tried to treat the trailer as a disposable item that would necessarily survive a few days of riding, without considering that in reality the riding in question is at the extreme end of what it was designed for.

Just beyond the river crossing, there's a rough turf bank with the remains of a cluster of shieling huts before a good estate track starts up again. It's impossible to plot a route across our hills on an OS map without coming upon shielings. They are the remnants of a farming system common across the Highlands until the people were cleared out to make way for sheep. Cattle were moved to high ground in spring and the people followed them to make cheese and butter through the summer, living in rough stone and turf shelters whose remains litter hillsides right across the country, sometimes in wild, high places but always, like here, close to a good source of water. I did learn about a similar system in school, but it was the *transhumance* of the French Alps, not our own uplands.

Without any fanfare we have left the territory of Astel Ltd and passed into territory owned by the Compania Financiera Waterville, SA, of El Dorado in Panama. There must be good reasons why Loch Garry and the surrounding land should be owned by such a company, but I can't quite imagine what they are.

The track undulates along the shore of Loch Garry, a classic ribbon loch through steep hills. The east side of the loch is particularly impressive, a steep, bare and featureless bluff with one windblasted tree silhouetted high up. The shore of the loch is, just like at Loch Lyon, a buff band of rocks and gravel about five metres wide. The reason for that becomes clear after a few hundred metres as we crest a rise to discover a blank white concrete building set back from the loch and, on the other side of the track, a huge sluice gate complete with a kind of mechanical rake to scrape debris from the inlet. There's a control cabin, but given the addition of a video camera and lighting, it looks like the installation can be controlled

Looking north up Loch Etive

South end of the Lairig Ghallabhaich

The Coire Beith at the head of Glen Kinglass

Cascade on the Eas Eoghannan falls

Ancient tree stumps above Loch Lyon

The climb out of Glen Noe

Lochan Uaine

Craiganour Forest

Gaick Pass

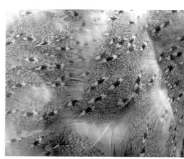

Crossing the Edendon Water; feathers and talons of a barn owl

Gate leading to the Black Wood of Rannoch

Campsite above Grantown on Spey

Abernethy Forest (above); Findhorn Beach (overleaf)

remotely. Strolling back to land off the gantry, with my hand running along the guard rail, it's clear that a bullet has punched right through the thick steel tubing, the exit hole surrounded by a neat flowering of ballistic petals. El Dorado, indeed. It's likely just the trace of someone sighting-in a deer rifle from further up the loch, but it's a brutal reminder of the sheer power of these weapons. My eyes flick up along the shore despite myself, on the lookout for snipers in the heather.

An explanation for this unexpected industrial hardware comes courtesy of a plaque on the blockhouse. The tunnel inlet is part of the great Grampian hydroelectric scheme whose construction began in 1928, the first network to be built in the Highlands linking several dams and rivers into a single machine for producing electricity for domestic rather than industrial consumption. It includes not just Loch Garry, where we are, but Loch Ericht to the west, Loch Rannoch to the south, and Loch an t-Seilich to the north, all joined into a single catchment area.

The scheme originated in the years immediately after the First World War when the demand from the soldiers coming home for a better life was overwhelming and fear of a working class uprising very real. The intention at the outset was to provide electricity for the built-up areas of Angus, Perthshire and Fife, but the project stalled until the company agreed to reserve a part of the output to electrify the homes in the water catchment area itself. This social contract unlocked the permission of the state for a project that was also fundamental to the formation of some of our best-known construction and engineering companies – Balfour Beatty and Babcock, for instance – whose predecessors both worked on and partially financed the scheme.

Further on up the loch, the barren slope of the hill is broken up by a handful of informal woods scattered here and there – one on a bluff above the track, another on the run down to the shore below. The fencing round them looks amateurish and in need of repair, but there's no denying the vitality of the plant community inside compared to the bleakness and monotony of the land outside. What we're seeing are the remains of another period of thinking about this land; a little-known experiment in the 1970s by Ron Greer and Derek Pretswell, a pair of fish biologists. They were worried about the effect of the hydroelectric schemes on fish stocks in the ribbon lochs of the central Highlands. Because the water level keeps going up and down, nothing much can grow between the high- and low-water marks. Land plants drown and water plants dry out, leaving a dead, stony band where the insects that the fish live on can't survive. Combined with an overgrazed and treeless hinterland, the effect on the fish can be grim.

They asked themselves what might be the easiest way to check this idea and the answer was to find a bare loch with a willing owner and get a few trees growing round it. They were fish biologists, not foresters, and they didn't have money for commercial fencing and planting. What they did was a triumph of adventure and ingenuity: they fenced off what areas of heather they could themselves and just threw in handfuls of lupin seeds. Lupins are hardy and have the remarkable property of fertilising the soil they grow on. The next year they came back and threw a few handfuls of tree seeds around and then just left the fenced paddocks to their own devices.

The result is that, in what could be one of the bleaker and most scoured glens, there are now patches of vegetation intruding from a parallel universe – one where the land wasn't grazed down to the knuckle. You don't need to be a botanist to be struck by the vigour of the vegetation behind the fencing: a mixture of birch, alder and conifers over thick undergrowth composed of plants I don't recognise at all but which have made their way here and thrived. Turn and look at the moor: bare and monotonous. Turn back and look inside the cage: lush, rich and varied. This is what our country could be like if we wanted it to be. This is what much of it would have been like before the iron smelting started, before the sheep came and before this golden age of El Dorado.

There is no biological reason why trees can't grow anywhere here up to about five hundred metres. In continental Europe, cyclists and walkers are used to climbing up out of wooded valleys on the way to the peaks, and it could be the same here if we decided to make it so. And why wouldn't we make it so?

As a perfect comic counterpoint to this gloomy train of thought, just as we pass between the last of the two improvised copses, we startle a family of feral greylag geese. The two adults spot us from their vantage point on the hillside above and decide to lead their youngsters to the safety of the loch. Their kids are at the age where they *can* fly but they really are rubbish at it. The first one just skims over the track and down to the loch, rippling the tips of the heather on the way, but the next two clip the roadway just in front of us. With their weight and ungainly shape there's only one possible result, and they cartwheel down through the heather in a honking flurry of feathers and feet before getting airborne again. I'm pretty sure they're sweating heavily when they eventually make it to the water.

Leaving the growing woods behind us and crossing the River Garry by a concrete bridge, the A9 starts to make its presence felt, first with the moving dots of the articulated lorries and then with the unmistakeable sibilant rumble of distant traffic. As we advance ever closer to the churning auto-route, we're also getting closer to Dalnaspidal Lodge, the centre of the shooting business here. It's screened from prying eyes by a ring of mature pines, the irony not lost on me that again the benefit of trees is recognised by the very people who bear at least some responsibility for the fact that there aren't any on the bulk of the surrounding land.

We skirt around a paddock of sheep and a few tidy outbuildings and come up against the level crossing on the Perth to Inverness railway line, whose gentle curve as it winds up to the pass at Drumochter means that a crisp crossing will be a good idea to avoid ambush from trains hurtling round the bend. Nathalie goes ahead to open the opposite gate so that I can get the whole length of my rig off the tracks in one go and we arrive in the small car park where she parked last night.

Our stay together in the bothy has given me a bit more resolve and a bit more humanity as well. I had been turning into a machine for covering distance, but the touch and talk has softened me and widened my field of vision from the few metres of track in front of me to the hills around and the Moray Firth beyond. I still can't shake off the thought of the pass through the Cairngorms, though, and my farewell at the top of the steep stretch of tarmac that leads up to the A9 is a bit distracted. I know I've three days' ride ahead of me before we meet again at Findhorn and some wild country to cross today. The noise and smell of the trunk road above us is unsettling me, too; coming after three days in the hills, it is quite shockingly intrusive. Still, this is my chosen route and, farewells said, I set off down the cycle path that links Dalwhinnie with Pitlochry and without which road cyclists would have to go miles east or west of the central Cairngorms to reach the north. There is an estate track on the other bank of the Garry that drops down the glen the way I'm going but I couldn't tell from the map if there's a bridge to get back over lower down. I know that higher up above the dual carriageway on the hillside there are remains of the Wade road from Inverness to Dunkeld but I don't know if the various remnants are joined up enough to ride or even if they're rideable.

There's an element of the surreal in riding down the side of a busy dual carriageway after my time in the wilds. I can see the eyes of some of the drivers glancing sideways at me, particularly the holi-daymakers with bikes on their roof racks. I've done the same myself, wondering what kind of fool would choose to cycle down the side of a motorway when there are routes infinitely more palatable, if slightly longer, to both east and west. Now it's me dropping a hun-dred metres of hard-earned altitude over ten kilometres to link up two hill tracks. It's not a level of ingenuity I'd ever credited to any of the cyclists I've seen here, perhaps unfairly. I can't imagine anyone choosing to cycle this way for the pleasure of it rather than to get to some more pleasant place, but to be fair there is a bit of payback. From the road, the gorge of the Garry just looks like a heather-clad gouge in the land, but from the cycle path, looking to my right over the railway line, I can see the river as it tumbles through some really beautiful bowls and hollows sculpted into pink granite bedrock. A shift of twenty metres in perspective has revealed a romantic scene, utterly hidden from the thousands of people passing by, though quite how you'd get down there safely I don't know.

Then, for only the third time, I meet a cyclist coming towards me the other way. She's making serious progress up the hill on a conventional touring bike with waterproof panniers, dressed in road kit rather than baggy mountain bike clothing like me. Her top is in the form of a Saltire and I congratulate her on the choice as we pass, to her bemusement. Maybe she doesn't know we're only a few kilometres from the geometric centre of the country.

Dropping down from the gravel path onto a section of old tarmac well below the level of the motorway restores some calm and with it comes the thought that this is probably the very tarmac that my grandfather drove his Triumph Herald on during one of his Highland touring holidays with my gran. A flight mechanic in the Battle of Britain, I don't think he'd ever have worn a Saltire tee-shirt, but I'm minded of the yellowed poem clipped from a newspaper I found amongst his things. It praised the 'English flight mechanic', and he had very carefully scored out the word 'English' and written in 'BRITISH' in copperplate capitals in formal and emphatic defiance of that casual amalgamation.

Although there are quieter north–south routes east and west of the Drumochter Pass, this is the main route from Tayside to Speyside. If a touring cyclist wants to get from Dalwhinnie to Pitlochry without using this pass then they either have to go back north and over the Lecht to Braemar and then the Cairnwell before turning up Strathardle, or they have to head for the west coast by Spean Bridge, Glencoe, Crianlarich and Aberfeldy. No one in their right mind would take on either route casually and so when the dual carriageway was built there was a risk of losing the cycling link between Highland Perthshire and the far north. The dual carriageway itself isn't under motorway regulations and you can legally cycle on it – in much the same way that we're all perfectly free to set out from the beach at Montrose and swim to Amsterdam. Death isn't inevitable but you'd be well advised to put your affairs in order before attempting either.

The dualling of this stretch had the potential to be a body-blow for cycle touring at a time when it was still just the preserve of oddballs and hippies. Anyone who thinks cycle infrastructure doesn't get enough spent on it now would be left speechless by the attitude of the early 1980s, and the ragtag, artisanal nature of the path I'm on reflects the spirit of that age. It's a mix of gravel, ancient tarmac and timber fitted in where it can be, rising and falling with the terrain almost in an echo of the Wade road higher up the hill.

Despite the Drumochter Pass being the main north–south route through the Cairngorms for road and rail, the planners at the time had been quite sanguine about imposing a *de facto* blockade on anyone trying to pass this way on a bicycle. It was only the most energetic interventions of a few enthusiasts that showed how cheaply and quickly a rideable route could be produced. Machines were on site anyway, and the winter debris washed down from the hillsides provided the ideal building material for the raised sections of a basic path. The improvised and isolated state of the track is shown by the sign at its northern end: it is roughly spray-painted on a rock, in a way that no sign for drivers ever could be.

While it is possible to get under the A9 through the culvert for the Edendon Water – the river I'll be following up to the Gaick Pass and Loch an Dùin – I don't much fancy the deep, fast-flowing water in the concrete channel. Carrying on to the junction where the B-road from Trinafour meets the dual carriageway, I overshoot at first as my mind recoils from the vast expanse of tarmac and traffic revealed by the gap in the trees. Surely that couldn't have been the way across? But it *is* the way across and I double back to dutifully line myself, the bike and my wagon up perpendicular to four lanes of motorway-speed traffic.

Quite apart from the fact that this is absurdly dangerous, it is also just absurd. I feel like I'm operating at the wrong scale or in the wrong century or dimension. Dalnacardoch has been busy since the time it was the crucial junction in the military road network, where the road north from Stirling and Aberfeldy met the road from Dunkeld to Inverness. General Wade's summer 'hutt' was here. It became a Kingshouse, one of the military hostels placed every ten or twelve miles on the Wade roads. Once the military occupation ended it became a well-known inn, which in turn became the modern shooting lodge, hidden behind another rare stand of trees at my back.

I feel intensely vulnerable standing over the bike in a tee-shirt watching the river of tankers, freighters and cars flashing north and south. With a lull in the closest stream of steel comes the queasy moment to commit to a crossing and get over the first two lanes as smartly as possible. I think I now know how mice feel when you see them in the headlights zipping across country roads at night. I've driven up this way so many times without much thought but now, with one thundering herd of lorries behind me and another in front, whipping up a whirlwind between them, it's nothing but a bleak, offensive barrier to progress. Luckily, the southbound traffic relents soon enough and I scuttle off onto the rough estate track on the other side, happy to have escaped from the crossing with my life.

There's a small signpost by the side of the trail, and two signs displayed on it, the top one declaring the right of way on the ancient public footpath to Speyside. The lower one, added by the West Grampian Deer Management Group, is a thing of passive-aggressive beauty. Management of the deer through stalking is essential, it seems, to protect the landscape from trampling and overgrazing. It provides valuable employment. All this in friendly sentence case, noting tearfully that disturbance could be a threat to jobs, though I'd have thought it was the employers who threaten jobs rather than walkers and cyclists. It then veers into shouty capitals with instructions on where we can walk — if we absolutely insist on doing something so unreasonable — without disturbing the vital work of protecting the landscape and feeding Highland families. It then slumps bathetically back into lower case for a plea not to disturb the wildlife or workers here. You'd need a heart of stone to proceed any further at this point and game, set and match are secured with a final ill-tempered upper-case forehand down the line:

YOUR COOPERATION WOULD BE APPRECIATED, THANK YOU.

You would hardly know that the appreciation in question would legally take place in the offices of Hunting Stalcair Ltd, of Road Town in the British Virgin Islands.

I'm on a track that has served as a shortcut through the mountains for the whole of recorded history round here and I'm being made to feel like a trespasser. So I'm becoming less and less fond of this bleak place and its virginal British owners and I can feel myself beginning to dislike the Gaick despite not having even seen it yet. I'll be very glad to put it behind me and the sooner I set off up the road the quicker that will be done.

The initial climb is through plantation woods and a mismatch in the OS map and the actual layout of logging roads finds me flagged down by a family pushing a small child in a buggy. After the slightly unhinged sign, it's a pleasure to have contact with proper, tangible human beings and they give me the very useful warning that if I keep going the way I am, I'll just run into the new Dalnacardoch shooting lodge and a dead end. I feel no shame whatsoever taking navigational hints from a man in shorts and flip-flops at this point; I just want to get out of the wood and start on up the climb to the watershed.

Leaving Dalnacardoch Wood, the full bleakness of this part of Atholl is on show. My eyes fly around over the flanks of what don't seem to be hills so much as banks of sloping moorland, composed of rough grass, heather, patches of bracken, thistles and stones, and stretching up into nebulous grey cloud. With the Edendon Water hidden in its gorge, there is not a single feature to attract the attention of any passing human. There's an anonymity about the land that fits well with the brass plate on a door somewhere in the Caribbean that announces, or more likely doesn't announce, the proprietor. Nothing to see here. Move along.

So move along I do and eventually come to Badnambiast. Overlooking the drop to the river, it's a solid, granite-built cottage that's now open to the elements and a home to birds. It would make a great bothy with a wee bit of work and willing, but you'd need to be in dire need of shelter to spend the night here now. I press on and after half an hour the sides of the glen start to draw in and steepen, the terrain becoming more obviously glaciated, the track levelling its climb and allowing the river to catch up. It has a raw look to it like the exposed moraine might be builders' rubble from its half-finished construction.

It's quiet enough now that I notice the low-key buzzing, humming noise that cyclists detest and which indicates that something is rubbing on something else. We are a breed not keen on friction and any noise indicates a waste of energy and a defect in the bike. It doesn't take long to find the cause. The fibreglass flagpole in the main pivot of the trailer is being worn away by the constant movement of the plates at the top and bottom. This is allowing the trailer's structure to fold back and down, as it is intended to do for storage once the kingpin is removed. That, in turn, is allowing the locking pin to foul the rear wheel, and the buzzing is the end of the pin cutting a groove into the knobbles on the tyre. This is not good. The rubbing acts as a brake and will eventually cut right through the tyre, bringing the trip to a definitive halt. The next few miles are the wildest and most remote of the week and I really don't want to be ditching the trailer and cycling out to the nearest bike shop in Pitlochry or Kingussie for emergency repair materials. The thing to do now is to carry on as gently as possible, trying to keep the stress on the flagpole to a minimum, and hope for the best.

The estate road here is good and the river crossing I knew was coming turns out to be a concrete spillway above a weir as smooth as urban tarmac, maybe even smoother. From here, it's a steady climb up to the tumbledown old lodge at Sronphadruig, half boarded up and missing windows but still with a roof on it despite the weather nearly five hundred metres up in the Cairngorms. These owners, too, whoever they might have been, have understood the importance of trees and fenced off half a square kilometre around the buildings to protect a stand of what looks like old-growth Caledonian pine forest spilling from the slopes down to the house. The thought of this whole glen covered with trees like these nearly has me in tears, as I imagine what we could do if we had the will to restore the disused aristocratic shooting lodge as something more useful, to make the bare barracks of our masters live. It could be an inn or a bunkhouse and someone could stroll out into an early morning in fifty years' time to see capercaillie in the woods and maybe even the remains of a deer killed by a wild lynx. Right now, though, there isn't a living thing to be seen here, not even a meadow pipit.

The general sense of loss, sterility and gloom is heightened by the presence before me of An Dùn, The Fortress, an eight hundred-metre-high khaki-camouflaged limpet towering over the western side of the Gaick Pass, the tip of its shell just ploughing a furrow in the clouds. The form of the hill on the other side of the Gaick is less clear but it's certainly just as steep and just as high. The pass between them looks like the hills have suffered a savage sword slash. *Gaick* is Gaelic for 'cleft' and the pass is well named. Some optical illusion makes the distant hills beyond the pass look like they're dropping off the edge of the world and, with the leaden pall of cloud sitting like a lid on top of the gap between the opposing slopes of the hills, it's like I'm approaching a triangular portal into another universe rather than just Speyside.

There is an urge in me to just get going, to get this over with. On the map, the track crosses the Edendon and then re-crosses it only a hundred metres later, but I've decided to see if I can just push on up the east bank to the point where the river turns west and the ancient track along the slopes of An Dùn drives north. To celebrate this decision, the estate road deteriorates to the point where it seems to have been washed away by the river and then repaired by casually bulldozing a dynamited house into the hole. The suspension sets up its standard Wurlitzer repertoire of wheezes and whistles as it soaks up the punishment, and I just can't bring myself to look back at the trailer, which I can hear bouncing clear off the ground as it hits each boulder and trough.

Eventually, the track turns to ford the river and I push on, following an indistinct footpath, as I'd expected. Walkers don't ford rivers in the Grampians if they don't have to and it's clear that most people don't here. The head of the glen is blocked by a bank of gravel, which, for the sake of my entirely unobserved dignity, I simply refuse to attempt to cycle up. Instead, I stop to unhitch the rig, push the bike up and pull the trailer up behind. On top of this ridge, the full glory of the pass is revealed: precipitous drops on either side above the stark black waters of Loch An Dùin, skirted on the western side by a proper single-track.

Single-track is the second most highly regarded track for sports mountain biking after bare rock slabs. Riding a bike at any sort of speed over mountain footpaths demands extremes of bike control, physical courage, strength and endurance. The twists, turns, dips and rises, the roots and stones and mud, have also pushed the manufacturers to produce the bike and tyres best able to float serenely over these obstacles at the highest speed. Single-track is where riders gauge their skills and also where local knowledge of navigation can be shown off. To me, this stretch is both the highest of the trip, following the five hundred-metre contour round the loch, and also the most technically challenging for me, the bike, the trailer and my three tyres. I don't know if I can manoeuvre myself and my burden all the way along, but I'll have no qualms at all about getting off to push if that's what's needed. I'm not engaged in sport cycling, after all, and there are no witnesses in this wild place.

* * *

At first, the path climbs up the boggy slope of An Dùn, carving through terrain that looks like what you'd get if you trampled a mixture of chocolate cake and Guinness in your bath: a brown-foamed, grainy, peaty slop that has the rear wheel spinning for the second time since I left the coast. It always astonishes me just how wet a steep slope can be, the water seeping out of the hill like sweat to collect in a myriad of tiny, terraced swamp ledges. After a short climb through the morass, the path ahead is draped over the shoulder of the hill and gently down almost to the water's edge. Cut off from the view back down the glen, this is a place of desolation and isolation. A cold wind springs up from behind and the prospect before me is of steep, stony slopes descending out of flat grey clouds to the menacing and gloomy ribbon of dark water to my right.

There is no record of Wade or his successor, Major William Caulfield, having surveyed the Gaick as a route for the Inverness road, despite it being more direct and no higher than Drumochter to the west where the dual carriageway runs. Telford did survey it as a shortcut for the road in 1828 but rejected it, apparently because the hills now above me were too steep and the avalanche risk too great. As I make my way cautiously in first gear along the twenty-centimetre-wide track cut into the flank of the hill, it seems likely to me that the self-made engineer simply understood that this isn't a place for humans. I've been making my way through the Cairngorms since I was a teenager and I've never come across a place as unwelcoming as this, even amongst the high tops. It feels, quite literally, godforsaken. The narrow defile has the feel of an urban underpass at night – it may be a shortcut but it's also the ideal place for an ambush – and there's an air of menace here that's physically unsettling. I'm not even sure that blue sky and bright sunshine would do much to change that.

There are just places where the landscape and the air, or some other combination of factors, makes you feel immediately at ease or even warmly embraced. For me, the two that stand out are Iona and Glen Lyon, both of which called out to me and still call me back. This pass is the opposite, sinister and repellent in an equally inexplicable way and I'm keen to exit this dread corridor.

Picking up a bit of speed on the narrow path takes my mind off the unforgiving scenery and provides a little fun on the way, letting the bike run a bit, always on the rear brake, just to keep everything in line and under control. There are a few places where runs of scree have left the way strewn with rocks and I take the speed right down to walking pace approaching the next one, lowering my eyes to pick a course between the grapefruit-sized rocks.

Looking back up at the landscape, it's clear that something has changed, something is not right. The sky is black and the loch seems to have boiled into steam. Things have gone wrong. The notched V of the pass has inverted to a Λ. There's an unexpected feeling of lightness, which my brain struggles to fit into the new vista but eventually integrates in the only way possible. I say 'eventually' but it must have been pretty quick, given that I'm still airborne. I've gone over the handlebars and I'm in freefall.

The hill is steep and rocky enough at this point, and the path high enough above the water's edge, that it is definitely going to hurt when I come down to earth. The only question is how much and what damage it will do me. There are no good places to break your neck but this is definitely one of the worst. It's quite possible that no one will come this way until the weekend. There is no mobile phone signal and I am on my own, whatever happens.

The first indication of how things are going to pan out is oddly reassuring. There is a high-pitched ringing crack that I recognise as me landing helmet-first on a stone. It's the same noise I heard when I walked into the cable of the footbridge over the Awe three days ago, just much louder. I don't feel a thing, which is good. At that point my body follows my head like a sack of tatties and I feel my kidneys hammering into the ground, sitting me up for another look at the slopes of Creag an Loch on the other side of the water before my momentum slings me head over heels face-first down to the side of the loch, where I stop on my back with one shoe in the dark, bleak water.

I've fallen off bikes on steep slopes before and what I learned is not to look round too quickly once you've come to a halt. Taking a cartwheeling bike in the groin isn't something you forget quickly. That lesson well learned, I cower down, straining to hear the bike bouncing through the heather to take its revenge for being dragged into this hopeless place. But it doesn't come.

Opening my eyes and looking back up the slope, I'm about six metres below the path. I'm conscious and I didn't feel anything snap. The surprise probably helped, as I was physically relaxed when I came off. The bike is hanging over the edge of the path, pinned in place by the sheer weight of its baggage train.

There's no place for emotion now at all. I need damage reports on me and the bike and I need to get out of here. There is no more to it. Standing up gently I can feel there's nothing major wrong. My lower back hurts where it took the brunt of the landing after I'd pivoted off my head. I could easily have broken my collarbone, but I've got away with what's going to be a deep and long-lived bruise. I run up the hill as if I was expecting the bike to burst into flames and lift it back onto the track to give it the industry-standard safety check: rear wheel, rear brakes, seat post, cranks, steering, front brakes, front wheel. Everything seems true and free. I think I've got away with it.

It's with the knowledge that things are all right, that there's no crisis or emergency to deal with, that I realise I'm properly rattled. I feel cold and hungry, so I get out another two layers from my bag and put them on. I need to get away from the site of the fall for my own peace of mind so I decide to push on to the end of the loch before I break out the rations. There's no doubt that getting straight back on the horse you've just fallen off is the wisest course of action and that's what I do, after I've had a look for whatever it was that catapulted me over the handlebars but I can't see a thing. I guess it must have been a rock that's also tumbled down the hill but I'll never know for sure.

A burn drains the loch at its northern end and I sit and then lie down in the heather above it. The clouds are threatening and I put on my waterproof jacket, as much for the warmth as the reassurance, before tucking into a lunch of sandwiches and crisps left over from what I bought in Kinloch Rannoch the day before. Egg mayonnaise never tasted quite so good, and the salty snack is very welcome, as are the entire contents of the water bottle, freshly drawn from the burn. I couldn't bring myself to drink from the loch itself, but the burn seems fine and the icy water is good and not too peaty.

It takes about an hour for me to come back to myself, to integrate the fall into my own story of what I'm up to and where I'm going. I have a real feeling of salvation and rebirth on having got through the Gaick. The Alloway Kirk witches may well have been in pursuit and they may have grabbed Meg's tail, but I'm across the bridge and safely into Speyside.

The view north down the glen is wild and magnificent. Again, there's a real sense of a descending staircase of hills in front of me as distant summits appear framed by the flanks of closer hills. The mountains are finely carved and far more sculptural than the rounded buttresses of the southern flank of the *massif* that was my entrance into the Cairngorms.

The Allt Loch an Dùin is fast-flowing but shallow and it's easy enough to get across stepping on the tops of the many stones. The track heading down the glen towards the Tromie and the Spey beyond is rough and wet. The buzzing noise from the trailer is getting louder and remedial action is going to be needed sooner rather than later. I can't rely on the flag to keep this show on the road forever, but the sense of fun starts to come back into my riding, helped by the thought that I've passed over the highest point of the ride and, technically, on average, it's downhill from here to the sea. I never intended to be a mountain *biker*, after speed or exhilaration. Rather, I'm a mountain *flâneur*, strolling with my hands in my pockets where others rush by, and stopping wherever seems right to soak in the essence of the land, so the idea of gently rolling down to the Moray Firth is an attractive, if not wholly realistic, idea.

Down past reed-fringed Loch Bhrodainn the land soon becomes more humanly comprehensible, with a rare stand of trees at the meeting of three wild rivers tumbling out from between the impressive buttresses of some truly remote mountains, whose names I do not know and which cannot be frequently visited by anyone. The track melts into the Allt Garbh Ghaig, a positively elemental river reduced to the absolute basics of a mass of water braiding its way through a field of boulders. If the moon had rivers, they would look like this, and it's a fitting place for what I think should be the last outing for my beach shoes, which I get from the waterproof trailer bag before picking my way through the knee-deep freezing water, gently easing the trailer over each boulder before saddling up for a defiant ride out onto the nascent track on the other side to dry my feet and put my socks and shoes back on. Again, it's not a ford I'd care to cross in spate. This really is wild, remote country, though the sense of imminent threat I felt at the pass itself is quite gone.

Dropping further down the glen brings me to Gaick Lodge, a tidy cluster of whitewashed stone buildings and one of the most remote habitations in the country, where nipping out for a pint of milk must be fully a day's walk to the nearest shop and back. Passing the entrance to the lodge, the quality of the estate road picks up in a pleasing symmetry to the deterioration when I passed the entrance to Glen Kinglass lodge three days ago.

Because the surface is smoother, the bike makes a bit less noise and it's obvious that the trailer is having a more determined go at folding itself up after the rough descent from the summit behind me. If I'm going to make it out of Glen Tromie today, I need something stouter than the flagpole to hold things together, so I pull into the verge and unhook the wagon from the bike, removing the roll-top bag and fishing out the toolkit and the piece of fencing wire from the bothy's dresser. I've already beaten it flat and folded one end over to make a hook. It slips straight into the pivot and I sit on the whole thing to keep it tight as I hammer the other end of the wire down the side of the tube with a stone from the road. It's Cro-Magnon cycle maintenance, but it pivots perfectly and seems quite able to take my weight standing on it without unfolding again. I can't get it quite tight enough to keep the frame pin completely clear of the tyre, but I think I've dealt with any risk of a catastrophic failure by switching from the sublime Lion Rampant to ridiculous scrap iron. With the flag back in its proper place and a last glance at the mountains that I'm suddenly convinced I may never see again, I'm off down the trail to Tromie Bridge.

The lodge is at the head of Loch an t-Seilich, which on sunny days must have an alpine feel to it, ringed by mountains and grand in scale as it is, like a deserted northern Lac d'Annecy. The sluice gates and other apparatus at the far end of it reveal the almost incredible truth that the water from this loch actually mostly drains out into the Tay, despite the fact that I crossed the watershed of the Spey an hour ago. It's connected to Loch Cuaich by a tunnel and then by aqueduct to Loch Ericht, which drains into the same Loch Rannoch I left behind me fully a day ago. Again, this is part of the Grampian Electric Scheme from the interwar years, and the thought that men lived and worked here digging under this high, wild place with pickaxes, dynamite and drills is as barely believable as the thought of invisible subterranean connections through these hills is bewitching.

The glen starts to open out, with clumps of hazel and birch dotted around, and I'm intrigued to hit a stretch of unexpected tarmac that makes progress pleasantly quick over the undulating descent down to the Allt Bhran. This is where the famous Minigaig Pass, the summer road from Blair Atholl to Ruthven in the time of the Jacobite uprisings, joins the road through the Gaick. It's nothing but an interminable and indistinct footpath high through the hills now but again this must once have been a busy crossroads.

The track alternates between hardcore and tarmac for a while, keeping me on my toes as I swing down into Glen Tromie, which is turning out to be every bit as beautiful as I'd hoped it would be. Sometimes there are just massive stone-filled holes in the middle of a nice stretch of metalled road and it's just really good fun to crank up a bit of speed and trust myself and the bike to weave through, round and over them. I've got back the sense of play-fulness that I've been looking for and which is so important to sucking the marrow from any bike ride. I relax as the terrain starts to reveal a cottage here, a telegraph pole there. As I drop down into the strath and approach the woods of Glen Tromie, a rare stand of mature broad-leaved trees where the glen narrows again to squeeze between the flanks of hills on either side.

The effect of the trees on my mood is immediate and I smile at the thought that it's now more than likely that I'm going to make it all the way to Findhorn.

The buildings set back in the trees – Lynaberack and Glentromie lodges – are handsome but sterile. There's no one about and they look like they might not be inhabited outside the shooting seasons. My happiness is tinged with regret that this fine glen seems to have no one in it on a decent summer day. Where are the ramblers, the anglers and the dog walkers?

The reverie doesn't last too long as a sharp right turn and a steep bank of red gravel tips me down and out from an unfamiliar angle onto the familiar tarmac of the back road from Kingussie to Kincraig. I haven't actually decided how to get from here to Feshiebridge and the entrance to Inchriach woods. On the map it looks like it might be possible to follow winding forest tracks over the ridge into Glenfeshie and down to Feshiebridge. I also haven't decided where to camp tonight, just relying on the land to turn something up in its patchwork of woods, fields and streams. As I stop in the road to take a photo of the signpost pointing back the way I've come, one big, fat, cold raindrop hits me square in the face.

* * *

It's the first rain I've seen on the trip and I'm carrying full waterproofs so there shouldn't be too much trouble, even though I've never been mad keen on camping in the wet. A few more drops and a glance at the heavens convince me that it is going to rain properly and, just as I'm putting on my waterproof shell jacket over my windproof mountain shirt, somebody turns the rain dial right up to eleven.

When I was wee, proper stotting rain was enough of a rarity that I can remember a couple of specific episodes of it. Once sat in the gym at school waiting for it to pass when two inches fell in an afternoon, and another time trapped in the car by a wrathful downpour on summer holidays in Ullapool. Now it seems that proper British drizzle is getting rarer and when it rains, the water is weaponised.

I haul on my waterproof shorts and I'd have liked to get a fleece on, but if I take my jacket off now I'll be soaked in seconds. The road surface is frothing like a beer tanker has overturned. I'm not going poking about in the woods, where forest tracks on maps don't always match up to the reality of things, not in this weather. I'm all for adventure but time is wearing on, I'm tired and it really is battering down now like a summer storm on the Continent.

There are no rules on a bike ride. I'd intended to stay off the roads as much as possible, but my rough goal of getting to Feshiebridge tonight assumes an importance and an immediacy that I hadn't previously given it. That's become the mission now, to reach my vaguely planned campsite on the Speyside Way on the south shore of Loch Insh, chosen simply as a way of being in eyeshot of what may be the site of the seventh-century Battle of Dun Nechtain, where the invading Angles of Northumbria were lured into the mountains by the Picts of Fortriu and defeated in the marshy ground around a loch, securing the independence of the northern kingdom from the southern one.

Setting off up the tarmac road to Feshiebridge, there's a brutal phase change as the rain goes from liquid to a solid wall of water. This is rain like you see in Vietnam war films: hard, battering and insistent, except that it's cold as well. My helmet's no use whatsoever at keeping the rain from running down the back of my head and under the collar of my jacket, but for some reason it doesn't occur to me to put the hood up. I've always hated wearing full-length waterproof trousers over shorts – just something about the weird clammy feel of the wet Nylon flapping against my shins. What I've got with me is a pair of waterproof trousers cut down to knee-length. I've been using them a couple of years and they've been fine, but this onslaught reveals their fatal flaw. The water is running down my legs in waves. Genuine ripples advancing down my calves as I plough on. Where can this water go other than, naturally, into my waterproof trainers? I can feel my toes squelching about, but that only lasts for a few minutes until my shoes actually fill with water and begin to overflow.

A couple of cars coming the other way have their headlights on and their windscreen wipers at full speed. I do not make eye contact with the drivers or passengers. Their world is just not my world now. I've become an aquatic creature. Every movement of my hands squeezes a bit of water from my saturated mitts, and I keep moving my head around to try to get the peak of my helmet to stop the water from running down the inside of my sunglasses, but it doesn't seem to be working like it should. A quick check reveals that the peak is no longer in place, doubtless now sitting on the shore of Loch an Dùin after I went head-first into the scenery. The lack of a visor makes little difference, as the rain now appears to have acquired a malevolent, multi-directional, penetrating capacity beyond any conventional downpour.

I'm pretty dry from the shoulders down to my knees, but I can feel the lashing water sucking the heat out of my body and my scalp begins to ache with cold. This is becoming genuinely unpleasant. I'm not a survivalist nut-job by any means, but I am quite used to being outdoors in rough weather all year round. This, though, has a spiteful, aggressive quality that's making me feel cowed and betrayed. Quite what loyalty the atmosphere might owe me isn't clear, but this targeted soaking is unjust and unwelcome. It's as if, having got myself and the trailer through the Gaick, nature has decided that there is a bill to settle.

When a city *flâneur* is caught in the rain and his linen suit is soaked through, he doesn't keep on wandering the streets; he nips into the nearest café for a hot drink. I know there's a hotel and B&Bs in Kincraig just a few kilometres up the road and the thought of a warm bed and a hot shower seems like the furthest thing imaginable from betraying the ethic of the trip. Camping tonight is going to be unpleasant at best and dangerous at worst if this rampaging cloudburst somehow manages to sustain itself into the evening. I'm here for the pleasure and to try to put a bit of real meaning into each day. Camping will just be survival, and a switch is tripped somewhere giving me permission to look for a room for the night. In any case, I'd told Nathalie that's what I'd do if the weather turned foul. And that bruise over my kidneys is beginning to make itself felt. A hot bath wouldn't do any harm if one could be got, strictly for medicinal purposes.

Swooping down from the T-junction leading to Kincraig, I start scanning for accommodation. There's a water-sports centre on the loch and they have chalets, which would be perfect. But I also know there's a hotel at Kincraig, so I reckon I'll start there and work my way back to see what's what. I just hope it isn't school holidays.

There's a bridge over the Spey just where it exits Loch Insh and the water surface is boiling like it was being machine-gunned. I will be glad to be out of this, and the quicker the better. Even the short, sharp climb out and up from under the railway bridge isn't unwelcome as the hotel comes into view. I grind on up through the small river making its way down the road, the front wheel producing a decent bow wave as it ploughs its stately way.

I don't need to see a notice to realise that the hotel is closed. There are random bits of joinery lying about and the sign I remember seems to be gone. I have a knock at the door just to be sure, but it is deserted. Not the end of the world, but irritating all the same. On the way back through the village, I notice that the shop's closed too. That's a real shame as many of the coast-to-coast routes come this way and it was a vital supply depot. The path from the Feshie to the Geldie is really the only east–west route through the Cairngorms, and many people, including me, have stopped here to get food, beer or a newspaper.

Scanning the village from end to end, there seems not to be a B&B with a room free, and I begin to suspect that this must indeed be the school holidays. There's nothing for it but to head back to the water sports centre and I re-cross the Spey, the tension gathering between my shoulders in no way diminished by the wet patch spreading across them as the water makes its way down the nape of my neck, past my neck warmer and into my fancy merino wool top. I think my underwear is still dry at this point but that's by no means certain.

Parking up at the side of the entrance to the holiday complex, I don't even bother putting the lock on the bike. Anyone willing to cycle in this weather is clearly so hardy they deserve the bike more than I do. There's a flight of steps to be negotiated on the way up to the bar that serves as a reception, and as I start to climb I'm aware for the first time of the sheer ludicrous weight of my feet. It's like walking with lead shoes and each step causes a small squirt of sock juice to erupt. I feel utterly ridiculous and not a little defeated, a sensation that doubles and redoubles as I step into the warm bar, smelling of beer and chips, and notice that absolutely not a single one of the patrons is looking at me except the children, who know a drowned rat when they see one. *No wetsuits at the bar*, the sign says.

I ball my fists in despair that the hardy mountain adventurer of this morning has been brought to this new, low ebb, squeezing a cupful of water from the leather palm of each mitt which joins the small lochan on the floor that has drained from my jacket. A few adults start to look up in case I might be about to collapse or even be dangerous. There must be a bit of pleading in my voice as I eventually enquire if they might have a chalet for tonight and it would take a heart of stone for them not to have some sympathy for the drookit traveller before them, but it turns out that no, there is no room at this inn.

Proper Highland hospitality isn't dead, though, and the young man behind the bar, clearly moved by my resigned response and amphibious appearance, phones his uncle at a caravan park a few miles further up the main road. It's incredibly good of him, the kind of spontaneous and creative welcome that warms your heart and which is the instinctive response of most people to a traveller in need.

But as I step back out into the pouring rain, I know that I won't be going to the caravan park. Standing dripping like I'd just climbed out of a swimming pool as folk eating their dinners discreetly eyeballed me really doesn't fit with the spirit of this thing, and there is a stiffening of my resolve to take the weather on the chin. I'm carrying one of the best tents available, I've got a change of clothes in a roll-top dry bag and I know how to use my kit in bad weather. Looking for somewhere to stay is draining both energy and self-respect in a way that even the rain didn't. Instead of turning left back to the village, I drop onto the small chain-ring and crank myself back up to the T-junction to look for a path down into the woods and onwards to the shore of the loch where, surely, there will be enough flat ground to pitch a one-man tent.

I follow a footpath down through the birches and, before long, I'm off the bike and using both brakes and a fair bit of muscle to hold it back from charging down the muddy slope on its own. This effort brings on a bit of sweat, and the blackflies that inhabit every wood pounce immediately. The trees are soaked and every touch brings an additional cold shower down from above, which does not deter the flies at all. The woods get thicker as I slip and clamber down to the water's edge and it's obvious that there isn't room to pitch a tent anywhere round here without clearing a good bit of the undergrowth, which I'm not prepared or equipped to do. I can feel the cold, the frustration and the fatigue of the day's ride forming a corrosive mixture that's going to have me throwing a toddler tantrum in the next quarter of an hour unless I do something.

The same calm decisiveness comes over me that helped with the crash in the Gaick. I've been this way before and I know that there's a bit of flattish ground at Feshiebridge, just off the road downstream from the bridge. I make a decision that I'm going to pitch the tent there and laugh in the face of anyone who tries to stop me. There are a few houses on the other side of the road but I'm pretty sure that no one's going to see me and anyone who does won't care.

The path back up is even steeper and slicker than it was on the way down, but I'm on a mission and it just isn't going to get in the way, even if I have to stop for a breather on the way up. This really isn't a suitable place for a bicycle, and the trailer is very keen to haul both itself and me back down to the loch, but we all emerge onto the road eventually and set out on the last mile to Feshiebridge with steely determination. I've noticed before that the area downstream from the bridge is not just reasonably flat and empty but also absurdly attractive, with a massive Douglas fir standing on a rocky promontory overlooking a deep pool in the Feshie.

The choice of ground is actually more limited than I'd remembered as the area under the fir tree is criss-crossed with roots. There's a patch of grass with a large iron spike in the middle of it. That leaves a gently sloping bit of packed earth, which in better times would be rejected out of hand, but now becomes my home for the night. The tent goes up with the head end at the top of the slope. I'm not intending to leave the tent until the rain stops or tomorrow morning, whichever is sooner, and that means thinking through everything I'll need. Sleeping kit certainly, but also dry clothes, food and cooking kit. The trick is to keep the inside of the tent as dry as possible, and that means leaving as much wet stuff as possible outside. Shoes and waterproof trousers stay out in the rain. Nobody's going to steal them, not even for a laugh.

I can hear excited voices carry up from the river.

'Can you see the salmon?'

'Yaaargh, it's massive!'

Then a face appears over the rocky promontory, followed by a well-upholstered pale body, barefoot and wearing nothing but pink Bermuda shorts. I guess wild swimming is one of the things you do when it's raining like this. You can't get any wetter, as I've amply demonstrated. The pool does look very inviting, even to someone like me who needs a wetsuit to swim in the Mediterranean. The water is so clear that the bed of the river appears at once brilliantly clear yet fathomless, and I've no trouble believing that you can see salmon. We studiously avoid making eye contact and they move off as I race to get under shelter and the flap of the tent down.

Inside, there's an instant feeling of calm. It's only just high enough to sit up, so I'm cocooned in a yellow half-light with the rain drumming on the tight skin of the tent. I rush to get my soaking clothes off and roll them into a bundle at the foot of the tent. I've got a full set of dry clothes, including my fleece trousers and they go on, along with a big hairy fleece that looks like it was made out of a gorilla and is as close to a hug as an item of clothing can be. The stove goes on to heat the kettle and I get into the sleeping bag to wait for it to boil, getting wired into a cold packet of pre-cooked lentils in tomato sauce which were meant to have been for lunch. They taste incredible and I can feel my body sucking them from my stomach into my bloodstream almost instantly. The coffee, when it comes, instant and out of a tin mug, tastes just as good and I can feel the physical heat of it being washed round my core, making me wonder if I might have been a bit colder than I thought. The food and the sheer relief of being out of the driving rain seem to erase the anxieties and irritations of the last sodden, freezing hour. Sleep takes hold of me like a pair of big hairy arms. I have no choice in the matter and I'm out in seconds.

Waking up an hour later I can feel the heat in the sleeping bag and the return of my humanity. I'm really pleased that I stopped looking for a room for the night and just trusted the equipment and the skills I'd brought with me through the hills. It feels right to have taken my soaking and dealt with it. There's an aspect to the trip of accepting and exploring my own insignificance in the face of the landscape and the weather. This feels like an equitable deal for my lucky escape in the Gaick. I could very easily be in hospital with a broken collarbone, but instead I'm hunkered down in a warm tent at a beauty spot. It feels like I've paid my dues to the various witches and goblins, and there's real satisfaction in coming through what was always likely to be the most testing day with nothing more than bruises and wet pants.

I've been carrying one boil-in-the bag meal for moments just like this. Chicken curry and rice, and it goes on the heat, both as a celebration of just having got here and also as the easiest way to get hot calories inside me. Adding the wine left over from the bothy into the mix makes the tent feel like a childhood den made from sofa cushions. What have I done today except gone out to play on my bike, got a scare, built a den and had a feast? And despite this simplicity, it feels like a day with real meaning.

Five

Badenoch

A long day in the hills capped by a thorough drenching left me exhausted and asleep well before what little light leaking through the rainclouds had faded. It's no surprise, then, that I'm up and about around six. The rain has cleared overnight, leaving the whole river valley glistening as it drip-dries in the morning sun. Slipping on my still sodden shoes, without bothering with socks, I take a seat on a rock beside the imposing trunk of the Douglas fir to see what the river is like after a night of rain. It's nowhere near full but most people would still think twice before going for a dip today, the flow surely three times faster than yesterday, the stones on the riverbed rippling in the optic of unseen eddies.

The morning is so fine and still I can actually feel the mass of cold air running with the river as a draught against my cheek. As I become aware of this gentle wind, I also notice that I'm surrounded by goldcrests – tiny warblers – at first only by their high metallic contact calls that sound just like the noise of a rusty bike chain. And then, as I let my eyes adjust, I can see them meticulously working the branches of the fir above me, foraging for spiders and ants. This, I decide on the spot, will be another good day with some sense to it, a direction beyond the line on the map.

Before I can get under way, there are the usual routine tasks to be done, but I'll also have to deal with kit soaked in yesterday's rain. With virtually no wind, getting anything dried is likely to be entirely futile, but I spread out my shorts and socks on the guy lines of the tent and my sleeping mat on the bike. The cycling shorts I'd taken into the sleeping bag with me to dry are not actually too bad.

Taking wet clothes into your bag and letting body heat dry them out is something I learned from a label stitched into the first sleeping bag I ever used, an American army surplus model from the Korean War. This is the first time I've had to do it in the thirty-five years since I first read it, and I remember distinctly realising just why the label had been placed there: for young men so scared they'd forgotten their basic training. Even then I was touched that someone had just thought the extra effort of placing a label where it might be stumbled on by a cold, wet, scared young man was worth it.

I've always prized variety and possibilities in life over plans and routine, but in the morning I do like to keep to my habits while I get used to things again after the other world of sleep. After the kettle has been boiled for the coffee, the beans and sausage go on to heat, with the brown sauce, salt and paprika shifting the balance far enough from toddler to adult to make them edible. Sat on my rock for breakfast, I can't quite believe I've got a roadside beauty spot to myself – the bridge, the rocky outcrop over the shady pool and the huge fir make a shortbread tin scene and my mood rises back to the optimism I felt before the rain came on.

On the way here last night I passed a Forestry Commission picnic site a hundred metres short of my campsite and they sometimes have toilets, so I wander off down the riverside path for a look. There don't seem to be any, but by way of compensation I do find a perfectly sealed packet of paper tissues, which comes in handy fifty metres further into the undergrowth. I have dispensed with any anxiety on the subject and this, too, has become mechanical and routine. I've shed another layer of city dweller to reveal the traveller underneath, not so distant from my forebears who passed right here on the drove road until a couple of hundred years ago on the way to Deeside by Glen Geldie.

The hot water from the pot where I heated the boil-in-the-bag beans serves for a quick wash and it's time to pack up. Most of my stuff is still damp, but it'll have to do. Clothes are a bit clammy to put on but they'll dry out from the heat of my body as I cycle, and I hope to get my sleeping bag aired this evening. Fully two hours ahead of my usual schedule I'm casting an eye around for any litter I might have missed and ruffling up the grass where the tent was, to erase the last trace of my stay. I don't think a single car has been past yet, and if I didn't know that absolutely nothing goes unremarked in the countryside I could almost believe that the locals might not know that I spent the night on their picnic spot.

The track into the forest peels off the tarmac road just fifty metres above the bridge, first up what looks like someone's driveway, before cutting across the tarmac road that carries on up the right bank of the Feshie and plunging into Inshriach Forest. As commercial plantations go, it's not unattractive, with mature, well-spaced trees. I'm moving quickly and quietly over the well-made forest roads, quick and quiet enough to startle a couple of small herds of deer grazing quietly in the cool morning sun. The wood is a maze and the forest roads on the map bear little, if any, relation to the ones on the ground, so I stow the map and start navigating by the lie of the land. I know I want to go downhill and to my right to find the track that goes through the deer fence and carries on to Loch an Eilein, and I just follow my nose and instincts, choosing the right turn and the lower road at the many T-junctions when I can. I really do not have a care in the world at this point, beyond the slight humming noise still coming from the tyre of the trailer where it's fouling the frame. I'm not even all that concerned about the tyre any more, figuring that I might make it to the sea before the carcass ruptures.

That this is publicly owned land and not a shooting estate is obvious, not just by the presence of deer and trees together, but by the fact that I start to see pine marten scat, which in turn means that I might see a red squirrel. Their ranges coincide almost perfectly because red squirrels are so light they can take refuge from pine martens at the tips of branches, unlike their fat American cousins who would otherwise push them out. Sometimes it pays to be small and nimble.

The passage of somehow identical but perfectly distinct blocks of trees is hypnotic to the point where I've actually no idea how far I've come or how long I've been riding. I could be going in circles without sight of a summit to orient myself, but I don't mind, so glorious is the morning and the smell of the waking forest. Swinging around yet another curve in the road something about a wee path dodging down through a thicket to my right just has the look of an onward track. Ducking down and bobbing to avoid a face-full of forest, I emerge into the wild ground outside the deer fence. The change in ambiance is instant, from manicured to something more like a curated version of wildness. There are birch and juniper along with the conifers, and the path narrows down and develops a bit of character.

The rain must have been as heavy during the night as it was in the evening and may only just have stopped, by the look of things. The track is deep-cut and narrow, rising and falling over the ridges, each dip a basin of peaty water. There is a ridiculous amount of pleasure in dropping the bike and trailer down into the flooded hollows, the water well over the cranks and just ambling through in bottom gear like a tank going through trenches. This isn't mountain biking in any sporting sense. It's slow and deliberate and cautious and I'm focused on the noise of the spokes as they beat at the still water like the blades of a paddle steamer, resonating in the tyres and wheels and right through the frame.

This is Monday morning, the moment so many of us dread and I promise myself never to forget the extraordinary feeling of privilege at not just being alive and well enough to do this, but of having literally nowhere to go today except to cross some of the most beautiful countryside on Earth. And, what's more, to have it all to myself. The challenge is perfectly calibrated – it's hard going to the point where it's entirely possible I'll fall into a pond or a juniper bush, but I reckon I can get there if I apply myself. These northern slopes of the Cairngorms are welcoming and comfortable in a way that suggests that someone has tried to make this a place that is everything the cold heart of the Gaick is not.

Although I'd thought the last ford was back at the Allt Garbh Ghaig yesterday, it seems there's at least one more: the Allt Coire Follais, a boisterous little river running strongly with last night's rain off the forested hillside. I don't bother with the beach shoes since my trainers are pretty much saturated. I likely won't need them again until I hit the beach at Findhorn and it's a thought that both heartens and saddens. I have become a traveller at just the point where the end of the journey becomes a real prospect. It's who I am now and I'll miss this person when he's gone or, more likely, until he's back again.

Moving on, the land gradually takes on a more tended, park-like feel as Lochan an Eilein nears. This really is tourist land and looking back from the immaculate beaten gravel track into the scrub from which I've just emerged, I spot today's sign facing out at me: *Path not maintained*. I can vouch for that fact and there's no harm in it. Who wants to live in a world where all the obstacles have been smoothed away? Still, I'm amused to try to imagine what could have prompted the need for such a sign. Maybe it was a pristine visitor emerging indignant, filthy and bloodied after a wrong turn off the manicured path? The track I'm on now is the historical route of the Thieves' Road, used by raiders from Lochaber heading for the cattle country of Moray – and doubtless *vice-versa* – before the soldiers on the Wade roads cut them off. Its exact course is unknown, just like all of the tracks prior to Wade, but it came this way and over Ryvoan to Abernethy, just as I will. It's taken just three hundred years to bring health and safety signage to the haunt of heavily armed bandits.

Passing by the lochan and its dog walkers, the path sets out again through wilder land, which is almost overwhelmingly beautiful. Mature pines scattered in rolling heather with juniper and birch and even a few reed-beds thrown in, all this with the north-western foothills of the Cairngorms as a background. The perfume is delicious, a mixture of pine resin and sandy rain-damped earth and that crisp green Nordic odour of birch. If there is any place on Earth that smells better than here, I want to know where it is.

The Cairngorm Club bridge is one of a handful that keep this massif open to those unwilling to wade. It is a vital link in the path through the Lairig Ghru pass from Speyside to Deeside and will save me a few miles of tarmac at the modest price of lugging my kit up the eight steps to the deck raised safely out of the way of the winter floods. The bike goes over first and then the trailer, which I'm finally getting the hang of wrestling onto a straight line. Banging that load down the steps at the other end of the bridge, I'm delighted to meet a Glaswegian family out for a cycle ride, the first I've come across since Kinloch Rannoch.

They're on what the guy calls a random tour out of Coylumbridge, a couple of kilometres downstream towards Aviemore. I can't think of anything better to do round here than to go on a random tour with your kids, just poke about on bicycles and get a feel for the place. They seem not to be bothered about getting lost, but like a lot of city dwellers they're worried about midges and rain and they insist on telling me the forecast for today. It's not something I much care to hear because there's nothing I can actually do with the information. The news is that it's going to rain again at two o'clock in the afternoon.

It's the first time in days I've had any outside information to consider. Up to now, I've just kept an eye on the land, the sky and the water and acted accordingly. It's weird but there's an anxiety that comes with the knowledge. If I hadn't known, I'd just have got on with it, put my waterproofs back on or just pitched the tent and waited it out, depending on the ferocity of the onslaught, but the delivery of precise intelligence has me calculating where I'll be at two, whether or not it's worth aiming to be at the bothy on the Ryvoan Pass over to Abernethy for lunch at that time. I can't stop it raining and I'll know soon enough when it does, so why does the advance knowledge perturb me? I'm almost at the point of resenting their natural generosity, and that thought does not necessarily reflect well on the part of me that still harbours thoughts of self-sufficiency – even if that was the part that got me through last night in tolerable comfort.

I wish them well, and share what I know about midges in return, or in revenge for, their weather forecast. I set off through the wide footpaths of the mature forest, out onto the forest road in the plantation and onto the tarmac road that leads up to the ski slopes of the CairnGorm resort. But there's no need for me to ride on that because the Rothiemurchus estate, run very much with an eye on leisure and the commercial potential of visitors, has kept the old logging road in place parallel to the new tarmac one up to the pistes, allowing me to indulge my off-road conceits a little longer.

However, the change in atmosphere is as abrupt and tangible as crossing from a peaty footpath to a tarmac road would have been. There are holidaymakers, walkers and casual cyclists around, obviously feeling welcome and at ease. It doesn't take much to bring people out into the woods and lochs – just a campsite, a restaurant and a network of signed trails. It may be that the bleaker estates I've crossed on the way here don't fancy any of the money that's obviously there to be made in return for showing some warmth towards visitors, or perhaps they want to keep their vast expanses to themselves. Or it may be that they simply don't know how to show warmth.

* * *

From the Glenmore Lodge outdoor centre, my path is up and over the Ryvoan Pass, which cuts through the spur of hills that form the northern side of the mountainous bowl in which Loch Morlich sits. At four hundred metres, it's not high or challenging and it's definitely still in the compass of the casual walkers and cyclists from Rothiemurchus. Halfway up is one of the minor gems in the country's crown – An Lochan Uaine, the Green Lochan. I pull in there to bask in its simple but intense beauty.

Although I know what it looks like, my breath is still spirited away. Anyone who's been to the Rocky Mountains will be immediately transported back there when they lay eyes on it. For me, I'm back beside Jade Lake high in the hills behind Revelstoke. An Lochan Uaine is the only body of freshwater here I know that is actually green – or rather, jade. Fringed by mature pines and a red gravel beach, and set in a natural bowl, it is astonishing, totally out of keeping with the sober majesty and bleak menace of all the territory I've crossed to get here. The colours are eye-popping and the scale tiny, like it was a cultivated garden or an extravagant art installation, or even a portal into another universe. I can't take my eyes off it until I'm spoken to by a pair of friendly tourists from Florida, who are equally entranced but driven to share where I'm drawn to silent contemplation.

It takes them a while to get over their shock that I cycled up from Loch Morlich fully forty metres below and two kilometres away. Our own habits set our expectations for other people and I think they're probably proud that they have got here on foot. It seems vulgar to tell them where I've actually come from when they ask, so I make a few noncommittal gestures to the southwest and change the subject. It turns out that they're going to be in Edinburgh and like beer, so I give them a few pointers on pubs where the locals drink and take my leave, just as a group of young adults arrive on shiny mountain bikes that look newly hired. This land is beautiful, accessible and welcoming and it is fantastic to finally see people using it, enjoying it, even if their enthusiastic chat, good grooming and fabric softener perfume do make me feel like a salt-encrusted ancient mariner who's stepped ashore from a storm-battered sloop onto the quay of a yachting marina.

Turning up the hill for the last pull to the summit on the loose track, a change in the road metal signals another change of ownership of the land under my tyres. I'm leaving the Rothiemurchus estate and entering Abernethy, which has belonged to the Royal Society for the Protection of Birds since 1988. There's no shooting here at all and no commercial forestry, though there is some farming. Where the land I've come through was, quite legally, dedicated largely to grouse even at a cost to other less palatable birds, this is a haven and refuge not just for the birds but for everything they depend on.

At the summit of the pass lies the third bothy on my way: Ryvoan. It's one of the busiest and best known in the country, and I won't be using it this time round. I take a few minutes just to look around its tidy interior and make a note to spend the night here some time when there aren't so many people about, maybe in midweek of some autumn.

In the distance I can see the trail heading towards the Lairig an Laogh, the Pass of the Calves, an ancient north–south drove road across the Cairngorms that was supposed to be gentler on the young beasts than the Lairig Ghru and which may or may not, depending on who you listen to, be passable on a bicycle. People have taken bikes pretty much everywhere in the Highlands, but there's a difference between travelling *by* bicycle and travelling *with* a bicycle.

Cresting the summit of the pass, a black stripe leads right down the middle of the trail. It looks as if some vehicle had a leaky sump or a filthy exhaust, and although it's actually quite sinister and potentially a bit slippery I find myself trying to ride along it as I rattle down, across the open moorland and into the upper reaches of the reserve. I'd thought that Inshriach and An Lochan Uaine were beautiful, but this place is simply enchanting, a testament to what lots of our country could be like with a bit of time and good-will. It is the diametrical opposite, geographically and in aspect and atmosphere, of the Dalnacardoch estate I crossed on the climb up to cross the Cairngorms. Where that was treeless, barren and unwelcoming, this is so rich, dense and vibrant that I find myself feathering the brakes on the way down to get time to marvel at the old-growth forest that's been looked after with wildlife in mind. Fallen trees rot where they lie and the land is bursting with vegetation and birds.

It could not be any more obvious that this is a healthy place, even though it is post-industrial. The lochans either side of me, though overgrown with heather now, are the remains of millponds dammed in the eighteenth century to power the saw mills lower down. This was once the heart of the timber industry and the place where replanting, conservation and forest management first had to be practised due to the amount of wood being removed. The York Buildings Company bought the right to fell timber on this land when it was forfeited to the state after the 1715 Jacobite rebellion. Extraction continued, despite the small profit margins after transport south, until almost the whole forest was gone by 1830. By the 1880s, the hundred-odd crofters had been cleared, the land became a deer forest and the trees gradually returned, a process accelerating now that it's a wildlife reserve.

As I ride along slowly, filled with admiration, I hear a bike lock up both brakes and skid in the gravel behind me as the group of youngsters from An Lochan Uaine catch me up and obviously grossly overestimate my speed. I get the impression that they're junior doctors, chatting loudly about their trickier patients as they carve through the woods rather than soaking up the nature around them, but it makes no difference to me and it's obviously doing them a world of good. It's so rich that I'll bet they are completely re-energised just by being here. There's no need for anybody, least of all me, to resent their obvious pleasure.

Further down into the tall pines, the tracks become harder packed and, sheltered from the wind and any noise, it's like cycling through a cathedral, the incense replaced by pine and earth and fungal smells. My mind unhooks from any concern about the forecast rain, or anything else, and just drifts as my eyes scan the woods for the capercaillie I know are here and which I'm hoping against hope to see for only the second time in my life. The first time I nearly died of fright after stepping on one in a silent pine wood in Glen Tanar.

It's in this state of reverie that I realise that the track is fringed on both sides by chanterelles, surely freshly sprouted after yesterday's rain, a vivid sunset-yellow between the green mossy banks and the grey hardcore track. I'm so disconnected from the process of riding the bike by the simple joy of being in this place that I turn to marvel at the mushrooms like I was on a passing train. Experienced mountain bikers know that the bike goes pretty much where you look. If you look left it goes left, and if you look right it goes right, and if you stare at an obstacle you want to avoid you'll ride straight into it. If you look backwards while steaming majestically ahead at fifteen knots, the poor bike doesn't know what to do. So it's no great surprise that at this point the front wheel slips neatly sideways, giving up its last pretence at grip on the greasy, hard-packed trail, and dumps me nose to nose with the chanterelles. For the second time in as many days I find myself on the deck, but I'm completely unscathed this time and actually quite pleased with my new low-level forest vista.

A few drops of rain at the summit of Ryvoan had seen me put on my shell jacket. I check both elbows to make sure that I've not ripped a hole in it but I've landed pretty gently. Standing back from the crash scene it's obvious that my untoward steering input caused the bike to turn a bit and the trailer to jack-knife, coming round to kiss the front wheel on the left and dumping me off on the right. It's funny how the impact of the fall in the Gaick, where I was going at no speed at all but rolled down a bank, was multiplied by the menace and bleakness of the surroundings. Now I'm smiling indulgently at my own foolish inattention as I check the bike over and get going again with barely a pause. This is a good place and I won't allow anything bad to happen here, and that's just the way it is.

The track out to Nethy Bridge is long and straight and a delight, covered in a carpet of pine needles. At the end of it lies a car park and the outskirts of the town, with a real old-school charm about it, all granite-built cottages and houses with rose gardens. I don't know what kind of folk live here but they obviously live well. I'm back in civilisation, with a few sleek four-by-fours prowling up the hill on their way to the woods I've just left. The trailer barely makes a noise on the perfectly smooth asphalt that brings me down to the bridge itself and the centre of town.

It feels like I've been tipped out of a boreal paradise and poured into the more inhabited, gentler and agricultural Spey valley. I don't want to leave but at the same time I'm imbued now with a restless energy to keep going towards the sea and the end of this road. In this land of farms and fields, the paths and tracks become hard to follow, the obvious ways are tarmacked and a bit of imagination is required to keep me going off-road. Instead of the Thieves' Road and logging roads hundreds of years old, I'll be following the Speyside Way, one of our long-distance footpaths.

It was opened in the early 1980s and, here at least, took advantage of an older line of communication that had lain abandoned since the late sixties. The former Speyside railway dated from the very end of the British railway boom, opening in 1863, long after the Central Belt had been criss-crossed with lines for the transport of coal and workers. At the time, there was a small network of independent railways crossing lower Speyside but no line running into the more sparsely populated upper Spey, with its distilleries and timber. The actual birth of the line up the Spey was complex due to the various rivalries between the other independent lines, and the early years of construction were a disaster after the contractor they hired failed to do any actual work. Finally, in 1863, the line from Craigellachie to Abernethy opened, though the ceremony was marred by a row about some second-hand rails they'd used in the last section of track. But it got by on passenger, timber and whisky traffic until the Beeching cuts, finally closing for good in November 1968. The track bed now forms the path of the Speyside Way, a green lane on easy gradients where nature is slowly and slyly taking the land back.

The path is easily enough found in Nethy Bridge: turn right when you see what looks like a station building. There was only ever light traffic on this line when it was a railway, and it never got above seventeen miles per hour. As I drag the trailer up onto the old track bed and take off along the platform, hauling my brake van behind me at a decent fraction of that speed, I become a steam train for a childish minute. The surface is mixed but, being a former railway line, it's pretty flat and between the myriad gates that the adjacent landowners have installed at every field boundary there's scope to make decent progress, even if the Speyside Way website suggests this isn't a suitable place for cycling at all.

For the first time since I left the west coast, I'm crossing a mixture of arable farmland and deciduous woodland. There's a smell of cows and silage, and the growth of everything is lush and green, in distinct contrast to the hill and forest colours of the last few days. It's also quite simply gentler and more human. And seriously festooned with galvanised five-bar gates with a variety of exotic locks and swivels on them, along with a range of special passages that I think are meant to speed me through but feel more like the kind of devices you trap cows in to give them injections. Given that the whole path is meant to attract us to spend money in Strathspey, you do have to wonder if they couldn't get the neighbouring landowners to fence either side of the path rather than installing this wonderful world of gates and barriers.

In a few places it's obvious that the owner of the surrounding farmland has come to the conclusion that the track bed is theirs – which it may well be – and anyone travelling along the path is a nuisance. At Ballifurth Farm, which used to be the name of an actual stop on the line, a looming construction of silage bags towers over the path, leaving a sixty-centimetre passageway for travellers to slither along. It's always an amusing exercise to wonder what would happen if a particular encroachment on a path were to happen on an A-road. Would people be allowed to stack silage there or would the natural hierarchy of travel bring a phalanx of blue lights to clear the way?

Passing through a bit of secluded oak woodland, I'm delighted to spot a red squirrel at last. After the wild and lonely trek through Argyll and the blasted pass through the high Cairngorms, every bit of wildlife is deeply welcome. This one's tail is bleached blonde, nearly white, making him very obvious in the shade of the leaves. Much as I admire him, I'd love to think of a goshawk making its stealthy way out of the Abernethy reserve and taking him home to her chicks. Goshawks are like enormous sparrowhawks, so big in fact that sparrowhawks form a regular part of their diet. They're just about hanging on here, and are one of the natural predators of red squirrels, but they are only really safe nesting in nature reserves and Forestry Commission land. Adaptable enough to have colonised downtown Berlin, they only just scrape by in our woods and forests.

One of the toughest obstacles to travel around here over the ages, apart from the Cairngorms themselves, was the River Spey, which drovers and traders used to cross by boat at Garten, Dulnain, Cromdale and so on – or just swim, depending on their resources. As I approach the river I'm delighted by the telescoping of time, turning off the twentieth-century tourist path built on the bed of a nineteenth-century railway to cross the Spey on an eighteenth-century military bridge. There's even still the memorial stone on the parapet left by the soldiers that laboured on it, with the regiment and the date: 1756.

A great knot in the mix of historical travel threads comes together here. The imposing three-arched bridge needed a bit of reinforcement, and that work has been done using the actual rails lifted from the track I've just ridden as masonry braces pinned onto the outside of the bridge. It's impossible not to stop and have something to eat on the parapet of the bridge, just to revel in the thought of the people who've passed this way over the years: drovers crossing the river; loggers from Abernethy rafting down to the sea and walking back up again; Hanoverian soldiers; unknown thousands on the railway; and countless ramblers and cyclists on the long-distance path. Casting an eye down on the river from the parapet makes me thankful I don't have to swim or ford it, as even from this high up in summer it's black and swift and deep. In winter, it would be a truly terrifying obstacle.

* * *

Pushing on into Grantown-on-Spey, I'm still following the line of the military road built by Caulfield, which ran from Corgarff in Donside to Forres in Moray. For a few hundred metres it's tarmac, before turning off through a wood towards town. What is now a leafy suburb must have seen companies of redcoats trooping through for decades after the bridge was built until Jacobite feelings calmed, even if they have never dissipated altogether.

I've noticed that on every day of this trip I've got so engrossed in turning the cranks over, finding my way and soaking up whatever the landscape has to offer, that I've almost forgotten to have lunch. Man cannot travel by jelly babies alone and the afternoon is well under way. My first concern, though, is to get the trailer braced and stop the tyre from rubbing on the frame. I can think of two ways of doing that: either making a new kingpin out of threaded steel bar, which I might not be able to get here; or some sort of improvised rigging with cable ties to pull the superstructure forward and off the wheel.

Grantown-on-Spey itself is a handsome town, planned and laid out geometrically by the local Grant aristocrats in 1765, and it's just the kind of place bound to have a proper Highland ironmonger on the high street with everything from sledgehammers to crockery. At the T-junction with the main road it's either left or right and I chose left for no particular reason, stumbling on an automotive factor, not a daft place to look for threaded rod. The guy is friendly and sympathetic, but he doesn't have that or cable ties. He asks, in that delightful small-town way, if I've tried Donaldsons, like I've lived here all my life but might be slightly dim. What other reason could there be for not trying Donaldsons first?

Donaldsons turns out to be a classic, the epitome, the paradigm of country ironmonger's shops. It has that smell of paint and mothballs and polish and, as was never in any doubt, it has both fencing hammers and unbreakable rose-pattern crockery. They do have threaded rod but it's six millimetre where I need five, so I leave with a handful of the longest cable ties they've got, pretty confident that they're going to keep me going for the next fifty kilometres to the coast.

The nice Glaswegians in Glenmore had predicted rain for two o'clock. It has been threatening, but now, one hour later than their pocket oracle suggested, the menace becomes an onslaught as the heavens open again, led as usual by a couple of well-aimed drops down the back of my neck. Given that I'm in town and as hungry as any self-respecting cyclist ought to be after six hours on the trail, I nip into the Co-op for a paper and head over the road to a café, the kind of place where you can get a proper butcher's pie and chips and a piece of cake the size of a house brick. Any pretensions of operating with nothing more than the contents of the trailer went by the board days ago. Rather than a defeat of some notional self-sufficiency, what I actually feel is overwhelming relief that, instead of being outside in the tipping rain again, I'm inside with a hot meal and poring over the newspaper to get some idea of what's been going on in the world for the last five days. It feels like parole from my self-appointed sentence of austere travel, preparation for the release that will come tomorrow. It turns out, as I leaf through the paper, that nothing much has changed despite my absence – chaos and indecision still reign.

There's a French family on the table next to me and I tune in to their conversation, always on the front foot to see if I can't give them a word of advice or make them feel welcome here. Not everyone finds France an easy nut to crack, but when I worked there a colleague took me under his wing and introduced me to his social circle, something I'll never cease to be grateful for. Having access to, having lived in, and having assimilated another culture and language is a good thing in itself, but one of the most powerful things it does is to allow you to look at your own country as an interested external observer. I hope Cécile looked at France in a different light when she went home, but I feel regret again as I realise that it's a question I never asked her.

And what should they know of England who only England know? That's what I've been doing this week past, listening to my response to the landscape and the challenge, travelling unfamiliar ways to come on the familiar at an unfamiliar angle, the better to re-assess it. It turns out *mère et père* are just having a minor dispute about who's got the car keys and whose turn it is to change the nappy. Sometimes, the mundane is just mundane. The rain outside is certainly mundane, not on the scale of yesterday's spiteful, close-packed downpour, just normal Highland summer rain. It won't last and I order another coffee and sit back to wait. Some might think a solo traveller crossing the hills should be taking shelter under a tree, and that's what I'd do if I was out in the hills, but there are no medals for heroics here. My route took me through this town, and a café is a great place to shelter from rain, so why would I not be nice and dry in here?

The rain abates a bit as I get to the end of my coffee and I get a quick wash in the toilets. The most basic things have taken on their real importance over the last few days – water, hot food, shelter and keeping clean. The feeling of cleanliness once I've stripped and washed is delicious, even if I did have to dry myself Quasimodo-style under the hot air hand drier. With the pie, coffee and cake settling down, I am ready to head out up the trail a bit to find a spot to pitch the tent for the night. Like yesterday there is no set plan, but it looks from the map that I'll be going through wooded arable land, so there's bound to be a quiet spot somewhere up the hill to the north not too far from town.

The penultimate part of my route takes me onto the Dava Way, also a walking route on disused railway that can be cycled. It's signposted from the high street and easy enough to find as it passes over the road on a handsome granite railway bridge. The railway between Inverness and Perth now runs over the Slochd, a four hundred-metre-high pass through the Monadhliath hills first paved by General Wade with his military road from Dunkeld to Fort George. Before that section of line was completed, there was a proposal to make a loop east from Inverness before striking south over the plateau on these same hills at Dava, where the summit is eighty metres lower than at Slochd and the gradients easier on both sides of it. The line was opened in 1863, just a month after the Strathspey, and immediately consumed in the sort of Byzantine price and access haggling that's inevitable in fragmented private railway networks. The present-day line over the Slochd was opened in 1898, and the route over Dava Moor became a branch line that slid into decline, closing on the same day in 1968 as the Speyside Railway, which it joined at Boat of Garten.

This route has meaning for me as it's the line my own parents used to return home from their honeymoon in Grantown-on-Spey during the hard winter of 1963. So as I cycle along it I'll be following the same line as my embryonic brother on his first journey home all those years ago. Our lives have taken very different directions but if they are ever plotted out by some all-seeing, cartographical-genealogical demon then this part of my life line will follow the very start of his, separated by half a century, and this in a place where less than three centuries separates me from dragoons marching to put down rebellion.

When the rails were taken up on the Inverness and Perth Junction Railway, the land reverted to the ownership of the estates it crossed, languishing for forty years either unused or as a farm track. It was only in the late 1990s that a group in Forres formed the Dava Way Association to make the track bed into a practical walking and horse-riding route that might attract tourists to their friendly, quiet town. They must have been quite skilled at dealing with the estates, some of which I've observed to be keener than others on encouraging access to their land, but the result of the rough and ready conversion work has been to make a semi-tamed cycle path that would make a great challenge for any recreational mountain biker or hybrid rider. Dr Beeching's cuts may have infested our minds and roads with automobiles, but he did leave a few interesting routes for cyclists behind as he swept the railways off our land with his iron broom.

The tarmac road turns sharply under an old railway bridge and, as expected, on the other side is a sign pointing the way up onto the track bed and to Forres. Twenty-three and a half miles ... which means that if I pushed on at full tilt, I'd reach the sea at Findhorn before nightfall, but I am in absolutely no rush at all. It's a beautiful evening, now the rain has cleared, with that resonant clarity to the colours and that odd magnification of the horizon you get with evening light after a shower has passed. I'm really looking forward to just pitching the tent and wallowing in what is a very welcoming and attractive part of the country, even if it isn't grand or imposing in the way that the rugged Highlands are.

The track bed is rougher and more overgrown than the Speyside Way, and the gradient is noticeable too as it sweeps east and north and up over the hill. It's nothing too severe and I'm still on the middle chain ring, but I can feel my legs working to make progress across a rough and muddy footpath before the way dives into a cutting only a few hundred metres from town. The rocky channel has been so completely reclaimed by nature it could pass for a west Highland gorge, almost roofed over by the trees on either side, giving it a romantic feel that's light years from the gridiron town in the valley just below me. Emerging from the man-made ravine, the path carries on past the entrance to Castle Grant, which seems to have had a private station built into it, and across some fields where a short stretch of the way has been neatly mown like a domestic lawn.

After a few kilometres, the cycle path and the footpath diverge for a bit, with the cycle path following a gravel track through some woods. On my right is the most exquisite meadow, knee-deep in wild flowers and fenced off from a neighbouring field where a couple of horses are eyeing me with friendly disinterest. Some places repel you and some detain you with a gentle hand on the shoulder. I have most certainly found a place for the night here.

The view is magnificent; over the gold and green of the meadow itself and the crowns of a forest lower down the hill, and across the braes of Abernethy to the full range of the northern Cairngorms in the background. Hotels would kill to have this view from a bedroom balcony, but any one of us can just roll up with a tent and stay the night if we're respectful of the land. It is an astonishingly valuable right and one we should, and probably will have to, fight to keep.

I unhitch the trailer and, as I have done every night when I've arrived, I have to suppress the urge to put the bike out to graze. There is something built into me that expects anything that has just had a wagon unhitched from it needs grooming and to be put out to pasture. Maybe it's an echo of the generations of north-east farmers I'm descended from, but the presence of the horses in the field next door is making the urge almost irresistible, so I make do by propping the bike against a pile of wood at a distance and giving the top tube a stroke and a word of thanks for the day's efforts. An outside observer might well think I was drifting into the realm of the unwell by talking to a bicycle, but I am emotionally attached to it and it just feels right to offer a word of appreciation and encouragement for tomorrow.

With the tent pitched to make sure I can see the hills from inside, I get my rations out for the evening and just lie down in the sun on my sleeping mat in the meadow. It's amazing how sheltered you are just by lying down in heather or long grass and flowers. What little wind there was is gone, and the small amount of noise from the A-road only a hundred metres behind the trees is dulled even further as I just lie and watch the clouds go over.

My clothes and sleeping gear are still soggy from yesterday's near-drowning. I spread them out to dry in the warm, gentle breeze anywhere I can – the ridge-pole of the tent and the nearby woodpile. Even the bike gets pressed into service as a clothes-horse. Luckily, it's finished grazing and doesn't seem to mind. When that's done, I turn to the routine of feeding myself. There's a free-flowing burn coming from the hill above. I'd normally be a bit more careful about water quality and maybe camp further up onto moorland, but this place is just so attractive that I'm willing to take the small risk. There's water cress growing in the burn and I've a dim notion that means the water's reasonably clean. With my water bottles filled, I get the dinner on to heat and the horses pitch in with a rhythmic metallic serenade as they scratch their behinds on a fence, and everything is at ease.

There's one last climb tomorrow and then the sweep down to the sea and whatever lies there. I'm musing on that when I hear a lady hailing me from behind the tent. She doesn't sound like the factor sent up from Castle Grant to tell me to clear off. They could do that if they wanted by claiming they're going to mow the meadow in the middle of the night. It turns out that she's the owner of the horses and just wants to warn me that her daughter might well turn up in the wee small hours to have a look at them. She doesn't want me to be worried if I see headlights or hear a car. It's a lovely, human gesture of welcome for a traveller and also, I suppose, a chance for her to check out the stranger that's set up camp next to her livestock. Both possibilities seem perfectly reasonable to me.

While my pasta boils, I get down to fixing the trailer with the cable ties. Cable ties really are a thing of genius and the salvation of many cyclists fallen on hard times in remote places. I'm really annoyed that I grabbed a handful for my toolkit without checking that they actually mated with each other. It's just the kind of casual mistake that can land you in trouble, but this time I've got away with it. Once they're doubled up, the cable ties form stays that brace the top frame of the trailer and pull it forward off the wheel. They're tight enough to make a satisfying bass twang when plucked and I'm pretty sure they're going to hold for the run down to the coast.

With my meal and a bit of the Co-op's finest red wine inside me, I can feel the fatigue of the last week racing up to jump on me from behind. Until now, I hadn't been particularly aware of the tension that goes with the sheer effort of dragging myself and the trailer across the hills. Nor had I appreciated the wear and tear of the minor injuries that go with any hack across rough country. There's something about the prospect of my goal now being in sight that lets them surface and I'm suddenly aware of just being really tired.

I can think of no better treatment for such an ailment than to watch the sun set on the Cairngorms and have another cup of wine. With my mellow mood and the complete absence of rush or any constraint, I find myself hypnotised by the clouds over the high tops. Although they are blown steadily from west to east and seem to disperse as they go, other clouds pop up on the western edge to replace them. The cloud cap stationed over the massif has an existence independent of the clouds that make it up, which come and go with the wind. It's like I've started to see the world in time lapse.

Looking down at my side in this meditative mood I spot a few *Psilocybes* – magic mushrooms. Not enough to be seeing things, but it seems rude to spurn the meadow's gift and I'm keen to see if they might add a bit of colour to my dreams tonight, so down they go.

It really is time to turn in, but something is missing from my evening routine, and it's bothering me that I can't quite grasp what it is. And then it hits me – there isn't a single midge. Crossing the Spey seems to have brought me out of their kingdom. There must be some around, but for the first time since I set out, the head net has stayed in my rucksack in the evening. I really must be getting close to civilisation.

I don't know if the lady ever came to see her horses in the night. I was so deeply asleep she'd have needed to drop depth charges to wake me up.

Six

Moray

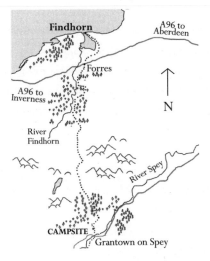

Around half past four in the morning, the noise of a truck grinding up the road to Dava drags me back to the world. The pitch on the meadow is flat, and the cushion of grass and wild flowers under my sleeping mat has made a comfortable bed. The pea under the mattress has been the bruise from my fall in the Gaick, which is brewing nicely over my kidneys and making for the surface, but it's one of those bruises where the pain from touching it is oddly comforting. The gentleness of the surroundings, the familiar dawn chorus and the knowledge that only about fifty kilometres of railway track bed separate me from Findhorn lull me back to sleep. While I've never been in any particular reason to rush before, I've always been keen to make some progress, to reach a campsite or cross a watershed. Today, there really is no push, no reason to worry about finding the way or making time. What could be easier than following a railway line that will be downhill after another forty or fifty metres of climb from here?

The inside of the tent is becoming a fixture now like it was my home; the colour of the glow, the familiar smell. The difference is that opening the flap isn't just like opening the curtains in the morning, as a different view is revealed each time. It's more like a theatre curtain rising and revealing the stage set for each new act. Today I have a fresh view of the Cairngorms across Strathspey, the relief subtly changed from last night now that the light is from the east.

The morning is cool and there's a brisk wind whipping the tops of the trees but I can't feel so much as a breeze down in the meadow. Somewhere in the undergrowth, a wren is scolding something. One thing I've noticed on the trip is the ubiquity of wrens. Tiny, unassuming and adaptable, they seem to be able to make a living anywhere from Narrachan to the Cairngorms. There was one darting around some exposed pine roots at An Lochan Uaine, and they've been criss-crossing my path all the way here, flitting from one stone dyke to another or just in and out of heather moorland. There's a lot to be said for having the size and agility to dart into any crack in the landscape if you need to.

I'm feeling less and less self-conscious about sitting on my own in a field and, as I put the trail behind me, I feel less like I'm intruding and more like I'm participating in the life of the land. The horses in the neighbouring field seem to have already been fed and that reminds me how hungry I am. There's a polished precision now to the passage of pots, pans and kettles, powders and food out of the trailer bag, into me and the litter bag and back into the trailer. It's only taken five days for this to become just as habitual as my daily round from bed to fridge to cooker and sofa. My trick of saucing, spicing and salting the beans is wearing thin though. My palate is starting to taste the absurd sweetness in the tomato sauce again and it will be a relief to have something else for breakfast tomorrow. There's only so long I can play mind games like that with myself.

Last night was seemingly the midges' night off and there are enough this morning to warrant the head net, but nothing too drastic and nothing to stop me dozing in the tent once the bag's packed. I don't want to arrive in Findhorn too early or to leave this glorious meadow before I have to, but at around ten the itch to get going becomes unbearable and I strike the tent for the last time, sling the binoculars and camera in my backpack and trundle back over the burn to the gate out onto the track. The horses are still scratching their backsides on the fence and I raise a hand to them like it was the most natural thing in the world, slip the chain onto the middle chain ring for what I expect to be a gentle climb on a good surface, and start turning the cranks over again, not without some sadness for the looming loss of my nomadic life.

There's a bit of a ripple first before the way settles onto the line of the railway, a few hundred metres of tarmac and then a turn onto a fine whinstone path through a mature pine wood, which smells glorious as it sheds the morning dew. There's pine marten scat on the ground again and my hopes for the day rise. This is country I've only ever crossed on the main road before, and I don't really know what to expect at all going this way. The map shows forest but it could be anything, farmed Sitka spruce or scrub.

It's not long before I'm back on the railway again and the reality of the path becomes clear. There are cycle paths in the Lothians based on old railways and they're either tarmacked or surfaced with fine whinstone. The Dava Way, it seems, has been made simply by lifting the rails and sleepers off the track ballast and letting nature install a green carpet as best it can. That carpet is threadbare in places at best, so I drop the chain back onto the small chain ring and settle down to as varied a diet of surfaces as I've encountered over the previous days. The standard fare is quarry battens, roughly broken stones that make up rail ballast. Where nature hasn't intervened and there's a bit of water about – which is everywhere given the rain over the last couple of days – it's like cycling through a pit of greased golf balls. The bike twists and slithers, the rear wheel spinning as if it's on ice. This is much slower and much more fun than I'd expected.

Sometimes turf has invaded the surface and bound the stones together. Progress is quicker there, but it's slowed right back down when the track passes through a deep cutting and the turf is replaced with mud, where water wells up out of the ground. I'd been a little apprehensive that this stretch would be so easy as to spoil the spirit of the ride. Nothing of the kind is true. It's rough, filthy and really quite hard going, which pleases me no end. I could easily see a poorly maintained bike being shaken to pieces on this stuff and anyone lacking determination simply grinding to a halt.

The landscape continues to surprise and delight with a view down into the gorge of the Allt an Fhithich and Huntly's Cave beyond – a surprise, too, to still see the Gaelic name of the burn on the map this close to Doric-speaking territory. The track continues to climb out on to Dava Moor itself and the surface settles down for a bit, staying as exposed ballast for the long, flattish drag up to the summit, where the original railway sign still proudly proclaims an altitude of 1,052 feet.

Despite the moderate altitude, there's no mistaking that this is the spur of a range of hills. It's open, heather moorland and the track I'm following is obviously used for access to the grouse butts I can see dotted around. Vast swathes of the upland parts of our country are given over to shooting estates. My transit of the

Grampians has crossed no fewer than twenty of them, as well as a few mixed agricultural and shooting estates. It's impossible to traverse such country without wondering just how it has come to belong to the people, companies and entities that it does belong to, and how come it's used for sport shooting rather than the many other uses that it could have, not least amongst them growing trees.

There are two main types of Highland shooting estate: the deer forest and the grouse moor. Deer forests are more prevalent in the west and tend to have rough grass for grazing and a reasonable stock of wildlife. When deer are shot, they're often gralloched on the hill, and the discarded pluck and puddings are eagerly scavenged by eagles in autumn and winter. Grouse moors have heather cover that is regularly burnt and a very particular lack of wildlife, especially any animal remotely capable of catching and eating a grouse. Many eastern grouse moors don't have any breeding eagles at all, despite grouse and mountain hares being a very natural part of their diet.

The fact that these great tracts of our land are used for the sport of the leisured classes is sometimes presented as a moss-covered natural tradition, but it's nothing of the sort. Stag shooting took off when the Parliamentary Roads opened up the Highlands in the 1830s, and grouse shooting is very much a product of two technological advances of the 1860s: the railways to bring shooters north, and the breech-loading shotgun needed to shoot hundreds of fast-flying birds in one day. Grouse are often cleared of parasites with medicated grit, and many deer are fed on silage and neeps to get them through the winter. Both types of estate are actually modern industries whose product is a luxury leisure activity inaccessible to most of us. Many estates try to keep trees off the bulk of their land, both to make the shooting easier and so as to qualify for agricultural subsidies, though I am perpetually mystified why luxury leisure providers qualify for those in the first place.

The other element that was required for the emergence of these estates was the gathering up of land used for smallholdings into a few hands after the Jacobite uprisings and the Clearances, as well as the legal structures that still allow land ownership to be so heavily concentrated. A crofter giving evidence to the Napier Commission in late Victorian times bleakly summed up the conflict between the crofters and the estates: 'I was paying five shillings dog tax to keep the deer off. The shooting tenant's gamekeeper came to the back of my house and shot that dog about fifty yards off. It was lying beside my wife and daughter who were lifting potatoes at the time.'

Families gave way to sheep, which gave way to grouse. Trees were felled for the continental wars, and once the sheep were on the ground, the forests never grew back. Much of our land is actually a post-apocalyptic wasteland, but one whose austere beauty we have come to appreciate, frequently from afar.

Alasdair Gray described our country as being an archipelago of fertile, habitable islands scattered in a bleak, heathery sea, and for the past week I've been island hopping and generally sleeping at sea.

On this last summit before I head down to the real, salty sea, I'm aware of crossing from the forests and flower meadows of Speyside behind me to the fertile plain of Moray before me. Land Rover ruts begin to dominate the track on the gentle descent and I swing the bike up onto the turf between them for a bit more freedom. I haven't come all this way just to follow in someone else's rut, after all. As the flat moor dips, there's a diversion off to the left where someone has built their house on the railway track – as good a way as any of ensuring that trains never run here again.

With the railway bed blocked, I'm dumped onto the main road to Forres in what is probably a bigger deterrent to family cycling here than all the mud or the loose stones. It's one of those 'oh, just sort yourselves out' solutions when paths and tracks just get too difficult – for which read, too expensive – and folk are just pushed out into the traffic to fend for themselves.

Here, I'm on a route that was made as part of the second great era of road building after the first military roads: the Parliamentary Roads. These were built from the 1820s onwards under the watchful eye of that remarkable engineer Thomas Telford. With the Industrial Revolution in full swing, it became clear that the roads in the Highlands, such as they were, simply didn't allow for access to get farm produce and people out of the glens, or merchandise in. A national project of road and bridge building was begun to improve communications with communities that were still, in some respect, economic enclaves due to the difficulty of travel, particularly outside the summer months. They were financed by a combination of central government money and funds from local landowners; with any amount spent in excess of Telford's estimate paid for by the locals, the contractor, or both. The roads that resulted are still the basis of the Highland road network today.

I feel both exposed and slightly deceitful riding on tarmac, so I'm keen to get off it as soon as I can, but just past a small warehouse unit there's a bit of hard standing for a lorry to park up. And there in the middle of it is a soft white and buff shape, motionless. Its form won't resolve in my eyes, and my mind at first has a go at imposing the shape of a cat on it before I get close enough to see that it's a very freshly killed barn owl.

I prop the bike and trailer against the bushes and crouch down to examine in close detail a bird I've only ever seen a couple of times, always fleetingly and at dusk. It's both smaller than I'd expected and infinitely more beautiful. The bird is lying on its right side with that wing swept forward, to reveal its snowy underside, and the other wing swept back. Its face is turned to the ground and its finely barred tail fanned out behind. There's no visible injury except a trickle of blood from its beak, and I guess that it's had a head-on collision with a lorry in the early morning – maybe even the one that woke me up – so fresh is the blood.

The feathers on its back are deeply, joyously beautiful; buff and white and grey and black in a fractal pattern that gets more intense the closer you look, as if it had feathers within feathers in a giddy spiral. I always carry a small hand lens in my pocket and I spend a good quarter of an hour studying the lush feathers and their menacing counterpart, the talons. Where the feathers are soft and intricately decorated, the talons seem almost to be designed to frighten – hairy, yellow and craggy like a boxer's knuckles, the skin covered in gripping nodules like the surface of a cheap table-tennis bat, and each one armed with a needle-sharp claw a good half an inch long. If you were going to design a pincer for catching rats, it would look a lot like this.

The contrast between the discreet pose, the soft, gorgeous plumage and the deathly talons is touching, and I know I can't just leave such a beautiful creature here to be mashed into the oily ground by passing traffic. Picking it up, I accidentally hoist it into the air, unconsciously expecting an animal so fearsomely armed to weigh about the same as our cat; but, of course, it's a bird and as light as air. I'm left with the feeling that I've just picked up a giant carnivorous moth as I lay it in the undergrowth under a bush with tenderness and a certain reverence. I've been keen on birds of prey ever since I was sitting in a tree as a kid and a sparrowhawk came and sat beside me by accident. It just hadn't seen me, and I watched its crazy eyes scanning around for a good five minutes before it took off. This is the first raptor I've seen since the young falcon at the watershed coming out of Glen Kinglass and I have been keeping my eyes open all along the trail. It could well be that some people don't treat our birds of prey with quite the reverence that I do.

* * *

Having made the detour round the house on the railway line, my way heads back onto the railway track through the flat heather moorland until it begins a long, shallow bend to the right to pass behind the conical Knock of Braemoray. There's a lushness to the scene as the track plunges into a sort of hidden dell with the embankments on either side thickly grassed. There's nothing grand or extreme about the scenery, but it just feels so natural and utterly deserted that it's quite beautiful. Again, although I'm less than a kilometre from a main road it feels like no one has been here for weeks, or even months, and to underline the tranquillity of the place I startle a roe deer grazing on the bank. It dashes across the trail to make its escape and is almost in touching distance, its tawny coat glistening against the deep green grass in the sunshine. Travelling alone by bicycle, you make hardly any noise even though you're advancing at a decent clip, and sometimes you stumble on things you wouldn't otherwise see.

The kilometres slip by underneath me and my mind detaches from pretty much everything apart from turning the cranks. The path has liberated me from navigation and the cuttings shield me from seeing the landscape beyond. When I'm up on an embankment, the landscape is flat and uniform across the plateau. This is cycling in its purest form. It isn't only the collapsing trailer that's slipped my mind – I've forgotten where I'm meant to be going and, in a sense, where I am. I'm not even watching the trail ahead to pick a line, just trusting the bike to run over whatever is in front of it. I'm both pilot and observer rolled into one.

But this hypnotic trance doesn't last long as my eyes are pulled skyward by the unmistakeable sound and shape of a military aircraft. When you see a bird of prey out of the corner of your eye, you *know* it isn't an ordinary bird by the heft, purpose and speed, rather than any particular marking; and, in the same way, there is no mistaking a military aircraft. This one is a Tucano, a long-winged, propeller-driven, two-seater trainer. It's caught my eye and ear as it performs a simulated attack on a ruined farmstead on a hillside a few kilometres away to the west, making a shallow dive at full throttle before turning towards the sea. It reappears to make the same manoeuvre not just once but three times. A little further on, the closeness of the coast and the airbase at Lossiemouth is underlined by the skull-like outline of an F35 jet fighter thundering its own futility at the low clouds. It's an American aircraft mired in scandal and confusion, renowned for its eye-watering price tag and lined up for acquisition here.

The featureless plateau can't go on forever and I have to start the descent across the Laigh o' Moray to the sea soon. The first and best fixed navigation point comes with the crossing of the River Divie on a glorious viaduct dominating the river valley and the village below. Although it became a branch line, this was built to be the main rail line from Inverness to Perth and the bridge is both solid and elegant, like all the bridges and even the cast iron fence posts along the line. The demise of our local railways has left a genuine feat of Victorian engineering to benefit no one but a few hardy walkers, horse riders and cyclists a century and a half later.

It makes a great perch from which to survey the lie of the land, which is now starting to feel lived-in and productive in a way that nothing else has on this voyage. There's a mix of arable land and forestry on the low rolling hills with a few settlements dotted about. This really does feel like I'm coming in to land, gliding back down to civilian life after a week in the wilds, though I know the exact point where that will hit home, which will be when I cross the main road from Aberdeen to Inverness.

This thought spurs me as I leave the viaduct. I'm still not completely concentrating on plotting a course through the overgrowth when I spot that the puddle in the rut I'm heading into is a good bit deeper than I'd thought. The water is the colour of Irn Bru and some optical trick made it look insignificant, when in fact it's deeper than any river I've crossed on the way here. It's far too late to stop now so I plough on, with the cranks and then the bulk of the bike under the water. The pedals slap in and out, and the spokes churn like egg-beaters. I'm getting up quite a bow wave as I steam ahead, impressed as ever by the bike's unflappable approach to everything thrown its way. It seemingly couldn't care less that it's now operating in an amphibious role. The trailer is likely to be submerged but I'm not going to look back to see. There are times in life when dignity depends on just carrying on a course of action that was ill-advised at the outset. And this is one. I wouldn't get any wetter if I stopped, but I wouldn't get going again and I'd have to clamber out of the rut sideways. That is not going to happen, and after a good twenty metres I crawl back up onto land like a fish clambering out of the Devonian sea on freshly improvised legs. This really isn't a place for casual cycling, which probably explains why I haven't seen anyone going in either direction all day, despite the gentle gradient and the scenic surroundings.

It doesn't take long to wind over into the valley of the Findhorn, a river for which I've had a deep and quite irrational fondness since I was a child. It was on its banks that I had one of my first ever summer holidays, and I think in some sense it has come to represent the whole of the countryside, and maybe even the country, for me. The Findhorn is also the river I'll be following to its mouth, and the end of the line, so in some ways this is the start of the last section, the last of the score of river basins I've been in and the last watershed I've crossed, though, being on a flat track bed, I've missed the exact point of that transition.

The feeling of travelling through hyperspace you get from cycling on canal towpaths and old railway lines – a sense of passing through and across things without quite being in the same dimension as them – persists. I'm getting a bit disoriented as the way sways back and forth between low, very similar hills and farms, so it comes as a distinct relief to find the way blocked by the back end of a Land Rover. Squeezing past through the encroaching gorse and broom, I find a gentleman hard at work with a saw and a pair of cutters, hacking back the vegetation from the verges that must be making the passage of a four-by-four tricky at points. I greet him in the formal, archaic way that seems natural on the trails and ask him what he's up to. He tells me that, although he's retired from his employment with the estate we're on, he has kept on working occasionally to keep his connection with the land.

'What we need are a few more roe deer to keep this stuff down,' he remarks, indicating the jungle on either side of the track as we chat about the wildlife and the countryside. It turns out that he knows the gamekeeper on the Glenfeshie estate owned by a Danish fashion magnate. The woodland on that estate has famously been allowed to grow back a bit through the aggressive culling of the red deer that were hammering any seedling that raised its head above ground. It seems that the culling hasn't gone down universally well with the estate's neighbours, who reckon some of those deer are rightfully theirs. No estate is an island entire in itself; deer are free to wander, and if we are to see more trees on our land, we may need tree management groups to operate in the way that deer management groups span several estates.

The conversation is as gentle as the man's accent, which is rich and familiar to my ear. I haven't really spoken to anyone since the family who warned me about the rain on the Cairngorm Club bridge, and the human contact is welcome, especially with someone who obviously feels such a connection to the land around them that they can resist the siren call of the sofa and the pub and come out here to keep the way clear for other folk. I do wonder what's going to happen with the collapse of generous company pension schemes and what looks likely to be a society where people retire only when they're unwell or unfit to do paid work, if at all. I'd be willing to bet that somewhere behind the project to turn this disused railway into a long-distance trail, there will be at least one committed retired person with the skill, energy and time to think about something that isn't of purely commercial value to them. I guess that in the past that role was taken by aristocrats and ministers of the kirk, but it's less clear who will be free to do it in the future.

Wishing him well for his day's work, I set off north again through the increasingly verdant and lush agricultural land towards Altyre estate. It's another milestone on the ride because it's the site of an early summer holiday when my family rented an estate cottage for a fortnight. I don't think I'd even started school, but I have a fair memory of where it was and a strong recollection of getting washed in a tin bath in front of an open fire. It would seem strange to me to just pass by without having a look for the site of one of my earliest memories.

As the way runs down the Altyre burn towards the Findhorn, it gets wetter and wetter and the place names lose the Gaelic flavour from the hill and drop into the warm, earthy and familiar tones of farming country. I've left the Highland Carn Biorach and Tor More behind me and swept down through the Lowland Ditch of Logie, Phorp Wood and Scurrypool Bridge. Even though the name of Altyre itself still speaks of an *allt*, a burn, it's obvious that English has long had the upper hand over the older tongues in this richer farmland and woodland.

The map seems to show a way into Altyre by the forest roads and I hack off to my left when I think I've got a decent fix on where I am. But this wooded country isn't anything like as easy to navigate as the hills, where open country and summits allow bearings to be taken. After a few hundred metres, I can hear the sound of chainsaws and smell freshly cut timber, so the sign closing my route for logging comes as no real surprise. It seems as rude as it is unwise to push on. This is just what the reasonableness test of the land access law is designed for, so I retreat to the safety of the former railway and push on, keeping an eye out for the next viable turn to the left.

There are a few hindrances still to be overcome in the form of mud-inundated impassable cuttings. On one occasion the marked way leaves the track bed altogether to climb up through a delightful pine wood, after a spot of hike-a-bike up a timber and earth staircase. For a brief moment it's every bit as slippery and sweaty as the climb out of Glen Kinglass.

The diversion re-joins the railway track just before a high embankment that crosses the flat plain of the estate farmland, and it's here that I at last have the chance to use the bell I've carted up ben and down strath without ever having anyone at all to warn of my approach. Now, I've got a party of three middle-aged naturalists engrossed in spying for birds across the tree-tops. They are foot soldiers in the regiment of well-to-do, north-east wildlife enthusiasts, and their uniform is unmistakeable: broad-brimmed canvas hats, lilac anoraks and stout shoes. Quite what they make of my get-up, I do not know, but they're highly appreciative of the cheery ringing of the bell from a good distance.

'That's a very good bell you've got there,' says the lead naturalist, identified by her gold bird-silhouette badges of rank. 'Not everyone has a bell at all.'

'That, ladies, is a bell with a capital B,' I reply, sounding the bell again for theatrical effect, which breaks what ice there remains between us nicely. They ask where I've come from and where I'm going, and this time I'm confident enough to set out the whole deal. There is certainly a look of bewilderment on their faces and doubt in their voices that anyone setting out from Taynuilt to get to Findhorn would ever wind up on the Dava Way. My vague assurance that I've come through the hills doesn't seem to do much to help. It's the first time I've said it out loud and it seems odd and slightly unreal even to me.

We get on to practical matters; what I'm really after is local knowledge of how to get into the estate from this side, and how to navigate through to the river on the other side. They reckon my map won't be much use as the estate woodland roads keep changing, but I don't mind navigating by that most human and reliable method: osmosis. Just keep wandering and take the likely-looking turn. Take the more alluring fork without worrying too much about direction or the lie of the land and you often wind up either where you want to be or somewhere even better.

At the end of the viaduct there's an exhilarating rattle down off the embankment to the minor road below, where I can just slam on the front brake at the bottom knowing that the trailer is pinning the rear wheel down. After a couple of minutes of tarmac, I'm back on estate roads and following my nose, as I don't quite know where I am. It feels distinctly like I'm following a spiral path that's gently bringing me to my destination, but I eventually come on the superb art deco farm buildings being restored as an annexe for Glasgow School of Art and get my bearings to set course past the big house, where the laird and his friend famously poisoned themselves a few years ago with mushrooms they had foraged, and out onto the main road. But I can't find the cottage where I'd rolled around in the dust fighting my brother for the right to carry the milk churn back to the house forty-five years ago, and I turn back into the estate with that memory untouched.

I make it back onto the Dava way through the car park of Dallas Dhu distillery, maybe the very last bit of Gaelic I'll see before the coast, which comes into view for the first time since I turned inland at the mouth of the River Kinglass. The Moray Firth looks nothing like Loch Etive, almost like it's not made of the same seawater. While the sea loch was glossy, black and hemmed in, the firth is greyish and matt-looking, but my pulse definitely picks up at the prospect of reaching the journey's end. At the same time, there's a welling of regret at the prospect of running out of land. I've become a simple machine for getting up, eating, moving sixty kilometres and going to sleep. The satisfaction I've had in overcoming all the tiny snags each day by my own efforts is beginning to be overshadowed by the prospect of a return to the intractable imbroglio of everyday life.

* * *

There couldn't be a clearer indication that life's grey necessities are about to return than south suburban Forres. After a last straight stretch across an open field and a mature wood threaded with mountain bike trails, I'm tipped onto the pavement of a 1980s housing development. It's nice enough in its way but completely at odds with the story I've been telling myself as I travel and whose characters are hills, stones, trees, tracks and maps. This is a place where the indoors reigns. The houses have built-in garages, picture windows and balconies that no one's sitting on. The gardens seem designed to have a mower ridden over them, but despite the American feel to it there are pavements. There are also street signs, which I find myself looking at with no little wonder and curiosity, like an explorer from another country. I'm still just heading vaguely north-east, following wide and deserted suburban broadways and pedestrian cut-throughs. The feeling of alienation is only deepened as I pass the high school and hit the traffic of the small town centre, but I can already feel the call of another of the waypoints I'd plotted on the map for this trip.

Sueno's Stone is the most astonishing carved monolith. I never planned for this ride to link the Tigh nam Bodach with it, but I was delighted to realise that it did. Their settings could hardly be more different. Where the Tigh is exposed in the wildest of glens, Sueno's Stone is enthroned in what seems to be a greenhouse built from the leftovers of a modern office block and situated in a suburban *cul de sac* in Forres. It's enormous, six metres high and no less impressive for being badly weathered. I always come to see it if I'm passing here. It may or may not be a Pictish stone but is often written about as such as it shares some of their motifs, but it is bigger by far and more easily read than any of the classic Pictish stones.

No one seems to be quite sure who the Picts were or what they called themselves. 'Picts' is just the name the Romans gave to the people north of the Forth and Clyde. Whoever they were, they left us a stock of carved stones covered in symbols that people have struggled to decipher ever since. My favourite is certainly the 'double disc', which looks remarkably like half a link of bicycle chain.

You first have to walk around the stone to get a sense of its scale before you approach closely enough to see the carving. On one side is a full-length cross, and on the other a great battle scene in four panels. The name of the battle is long lost, but the consequences are clear. There is a pile of severed heads, a victim awaiting decapitation and a line of vanquished soldiers being led into slavery as a king looks on. Of all the theories put forward to explain it, my favourite is that it was created on the orders of Kenneth Mac Alpin and placed in the Picts' land to remind them that they had been beaten and absorbed by the new Irish invaders. It's a tactic that some residents of Montmartre still believe explains the imposition of the alien-looking Sacré-Coeur on the hill above that working-class district as revenge for their enthusiastic participation in the brutally crushed Paris Commune. The basilica isn't quite as ugly as the battle scenes on Sueno's Stone but the parallel is tempting. A six-metre-high carved stone slab, quite possibly painted in bright colours, must have been an imposing piece of propaganda at the end of the Iron Age, whatever its function. To me, it stands as a monument to the constancy of both conflict and forgetting, to the certainty that our own battles, no matter how savage, will be forgotten in due course.

Just behind the stone, a pedestrian and cycle bridge crosses over the A96 main road between Aberdeen and Inverness and the elevated viewpoint as I cross it just reinforces the impression of highly efficient futility in the speed of the vehicles. The smell and noise are startling to my senses, still tuned to the flower meadow where I woke up. It's a short haul along a B-road and across the railway line to the turn down to Findhorn itself.

There's a shared use path alongside and I'm very happy to amble along it towards the Findhorn Foundation, a place for experimental living with turfed houses and giant vegetables, accidentally established in the sixties right next to the air force base at Kinloss. A Tornado bomber circles the base disconsolately, apparently unaware that it has been turned over to the army. For the first time in days a cyclist appears in the other direction, and by her Dutch bike and dress it's obvious she lives in the community. Her face is nut brown and she gives me the biggest, most natural smile I've ever had from a passing stranger. It's quite an advert for however she's living there. A bit further on the path peters out under the stern glare of today's best sign:

CYCLISTS DISMOUNT
Cyclists to Findhorn
Please rejoin
main carriageway

I have to concede that I am a cyclist to Findhorn, but they'd have to send a squad of riot police to get me to dismount. The Gaick unhorsed me, but this pettifogging municipal ironmongery will not. I don't seem to have any choice in re-joining the main carriageway but dismounting is simply not on the agenda right now. Dismounting occurs when you've got where you're going, and in my case that is the pier at Findhorn. They should have signs all over the place saying simply, *Cyclists Mount*. In fact, they should say, *Non-Cyclists Mount*. Everyone physically capable of turning the cranks of a bike – an electric bike, if need be – should be doing just that as often as they can.

So I turn my cranks over and admire the wide lagoon of the Findhorn, with Culbin Forest on the other side, and shortly I find myself freewheeling cautiously over the rough stonework of the jetty, mindful of the ridicule that will ensue if I fall off into the muddy lagoon. As I roll to a stop, the fabric of space and time is pinched up and folded for the briefest moment. The me of Taynuilt meets the me of Findhorn – lighter, dirtier, stronger. Those two jetties are now stitched together by a thread running in a narrow groove across the Grampians, and whenever I cross that thread I'll be taken back to this point in my life, this here, by the two hundred and seventy-kilometre-long tripwire.

With a trailer and a crust of mud, my bike looks odd and I look rough, so the tourists wandering along the village seafront are giving space to what they must figure is a tramp. That suits me as I look for a place to set the camera down on its tiny tripod for the shot that will prove in years to come that I was there and then I was here.

There's a certain numbness to it all, a disbelief that I don't have another sixty kilometres tomorrow and that I'll be sleeping in my own bed tonight. I've still got a day's food and part of me wants to just keep going along the coast. There is no sense of triumph because I've enough sense to know that I came for the journey, not the destination, but there is another idea, much more insidious, that I can feel hatching from its jet-black egg, and the idea is this: if I've completed the challenge then the challenge was insignificant. It's an idea that I know won't go away and in a way I'm glad that it came so soon. The main thing that I feel is curiosity. Curiosity at what made me do this and what allowed me to do this, and curiosity at all the things I found and the people I met. But the sense of having failed, through cheap success, will always be there too. It's a thought that hangs heavy as I set off for the sand-spit that marks the mouth of the Findhorn, the sea and the end of this journey.

Nathalie is waiting for me in the dunes and walks alongside me as I stubbornly insist on cycling along the boardwalk through to the beach proper. Her delight that I have finished the challenge I set myself is radiating from her, despite the slight confusion over exactly where we were to meet. I'd thought it was the pier; she'd naturally assumed the beach as there is only one way any coast-to-coast bike ride can finish. That's with the bike as close to the water as it can get and its rider fully immersed in the sea. Luckily, cycling undershorts make pretty decent swimming trunks, even with the synthetic chamois pad. As I strip off, I'm sand-blasted by the brisk onshore wind, bringing back memories about child-hood summers on Aberdeen beach. My face, legs and arms are quite deeply weather-beaten, my torso and feet milky white just as they should be on any self-respecting, rule-abiding cyclist. I am a fearful and easily chilled swimmer, but I wade straight out into the firth and, as soon as the water has wrapped its icy grip round my undercarriage, I just lunge out to sea for a few strokes, letting the shock of immersion serve like a baptism to bring me back to a new Earth. I stagger out onto to the beach, shivering and looking for the comfort of a big towel and a hug. I don't quite know what to think of what I've just done. I do, though, know what to do, and that's to get food and beer.

Parking my backside on a well-upholstered pub chair is an extraordinary pleasure. Chairs are surely one of the most under-valued things going, but you have to be outdoors for a few days to really know it. The conversation around me is overwhelming at first but that fades quickly enough and I set myself to making the acquaintance of fish and vegetables, both of which have been notably lacking from my ration packs, along with three pints of cold, well-hopped IPA. Salt water has washed the outside of me and beer will wash the inside.

The car is parked in the dunes and, as I dismantle the rig for the last time and stow the trailer in the boot and the bike on the roof, I get the distinct feeling of being watched. The car next to ours contains five perfectly white retrievers, three in the back and two in the front, one of them sitting at the steering wheel looking like he might well just have driven there. All of them are looking straight at me with their deep, dark eyes. The lady in charge of this canine formation arrives back and makes the friendly but rather unlikely claim that swimming wasn't a great idea today as high tide was last week, before manhandling the dog in the driver's seat through the gap between the front seats and into the back with its three comrades. I'm tired and I can't figure out what, if anything, the episode means.

On the road back to Edinburgh we pass the bush where I know there lies a new-slain owl. I salute it silently as we pass.

Seven

Edinburgh

It took me a long time to understand the sense of sadness that came over me in the hills behind Forres when the Moray Firth appeared on the horizon. Stripped of all the luminous distractions of modern life and immersed in the arduous but uncomplicated business of hauling myself from one coast to the other, I had regained the innocence of childhood, that time before the inevitable and personal nature of death becomes real.

For me, that reality had dawned when I was eight years old, on the morning that I woke up in the room I shared with my brother to find him gone and replaced by a wizened old man in his bed. He'd been a bit under the weather for weeks but became seriously, gravely unwell in the space of a few hours overnight. There was an ambulance and there were hospital corridors that smelt of cabbage and disinfectant, and there were strange meals cooked by the wrong people. He didn't die, but death had come to roost in my head and in my heart. I was a smart kid and deduced that everyone around me would die in due course, and I set about becoming quiet and self-reliant, the kind of child who would grow into the kind of man that would take off into the hills on his own with a bicycle and a tent.

When I got home from Findhorn, I had a bath and something to eat and went to sleep. I was knackered. I was weather-beaten and a bit lost. I had a bruise over my kidneys the size and shape of Ireland. I had a fine collection of cuts and grazes. I had the traces of three ticks, a gleg bite and a peppering of midge bites. And I spent the next five days in bed suffering from a wearisome and persistent stomach upset whose origin I have little doubt was the water in the burn running through the flower meadow above Grantown.

But, unlike my friend Cécile, I wasn't dead. Nor had I overcome death, but I had accepted hers and laid down a vintage of memories of a line engraved across the country, spanning time as much as space. These are memories powerful enough that I know I will have them as long as I live. If I could choose one to savour when my time comes, it would be watching the embers burn down in the wild silence of Duinish.

I conjured my journey's course from maps, which have always been magical talismans in times of uncertainty for me, containing as they do the solutions to problems no one ever imagined when they were drawn. The density of information on them is astonishing and the price modest. To spend an hour with a contour map is to roam for a year. Perhaps the most extraordinary thing is to stack maps of different ages of the same place on top of each other and dive down through them, watching things change, or more often not change, through time. Maps lead you to contemplation, and contemplation can and should lead to action. For me, the maps became like miniature portraits of a loved one, a soothing keepsake simultaneously annihilating and amplifying the distance between us.

The popularity of Ordnance Survey maps and the invention of the safety bicycle seem likely to have come about at the same time for a reason. Bicycles represent the best and cheapest way to unlock the landscape on the map in your hand. For a modest sum, you can triple or quadruple your speed and engage in accelerated walking – not skating over the landscape like you do in a car, but swimming through it with all your senses engaged.

Get it right and the machine itself disappears beneath you. Of course, cycling involves making some effort. The French have a concept of *oisiveté*, a delightfully cultured indifference to all action, which can be a welcome antidote to the modern era's imperatives of busyness, production and consumption. Drift and inaction can be pleasant for a time, but not in the long term. We are all on a road to the same place whatever we do, but we can choose which one. Travelling with purpose cheated death while I was engaged in the journey. The North Sea had been hidden behind the whole country when I set off, but I had ground away at the horizon inch by inch until it came into view. On the pier at Taynuilt, the prospect of my ever reaching it had been as unreal and distant as death had been to me as a child, but it became more real as I crawled over each hill. There was something in this thrawn pilgrimage that was deeply satisfying, the absence of my everyday self and the immersion in that single goal.

What was Nathalie's verdict, beyond the polite admiration due and proper to the whims of her partner? *Ce que tu viens de faire n'est pas entièrement normal.* 'What you've just done isn't entirely normal.' She was quite right, of course, but why isn't it normal? I'd found deep joy through the exercise of what ought to be commonplace skills – reading a map, riding a bike and pitching a tent. Our country is criss-crossed with trails and our garages, sheds and closes are filled with mountain bikes far more capable than the makeshift assembly of cogs and tubes that I ride. The full set of Ordnance Survey maps is freely available online, and tents are a disposable commodity abandoned after festivals. The Land Reform Act of 2003 gives all of us all the right to walk, swim, cycle or paddle on our open ground and water provided that we exercise this precious right in the only proper way: reasonably. So why was it I met no one doing the same as me from one side of the country to the other in high summer?

The folk that make television adverts try hard to give the impression that four-by-four vehicles open up a world of adventure, but, unless you own an estate, where exactly would you drive one? Maybe on the gravel roads of Iceland or New Zealand, but here you have no right to drive on any private road. Buy yourself a bicycle, on the other hand, and miles of track are freely available to any responsible rider. Buy yourself a trail bike and the whole country is your oyster and the forests the pearls within.

We live in an age of aversion to easily imagined risks. We drive our bairns to school to keep them from being run over or abducted, all the while exposing them to the far greater risk of learning a cloistered, inactive way of life, cut off from the knowledge that rain isn't fatal and physical effort can cheer you up. Anyone can conjure a whole host of horrors that *could* happen when you take off into the hills. You could fall in a river and drown. You could crack your head on a rock. You could get lost and die of exposure. But you can die of underexposure too. Maybe it isn't as visible and maybe no one tuts fearfully when you announce your plan to spend the afternoon on the sofa, but anyone with any concern for their mental or physical well-being should get out and walk in their nearest wood. The Japanese found they had to invent a word for it, *shinrin-yoku*, so useful is this concept of 'forest bathing' to their notion of a life well lived.

Some years ago a woman murdered her boyfriend a few streets away from us, shooting him in the head with a pistol in cold blood. She asked her brother to dispose of the weapon, and he in turn got a third local man to get rid of it. What he chose to do has always struck me as an insight into how some urban folk see the land: he buried it in a park, no more than a hundred metres from the scene of the crime. It wasn't a manicured park, right enough – it's wooded and there are roe deer and a pair of buzzards in it – but it's right in the heart of suburban Edinburgh. Of course, a dog being walked in the park dug the gun up shortly afterwards, a gun which hadn't even been cleaned and which duly convicted the murderers. I wonder if the man who buried it thought that he was in such a wild and desolate place – away from pavements and streetlights – that it might as well have been at the bottom of the Atlantic. What a limitation of imagination and a circumscription of adventure that would reveal. Could you get any further from *shinrin-yoku*?

We are getting fatter, sadder and less capable by the year. At the same time as we lionise elite athletes and extreme adventurers we seem to be losing our own taste for domestic exploration. And we are entering a time when independent thought and action will be both necessary and profitable. The catalogue of David Rattray and Co, a Glasgow bicycle manufacturer in the 1920s, recalled that 'when that unpleasantness was over, the reaction urged young folks to the open-air life, and Cycling and Camping became very popular'. The unpleasantness in question was the First World War. It is as tedious as it is unproductive to hark back to any golden age of physical activity. Many of the cyclists and campers in question will have been used to hard physical work and some may even have fought in the trenches. Our world is not theirs, but their reaction to deadly horror is instructive.

As I've said before, on my journey, I tried to have a rule that I took nothing with a single use; prizing, above all, things such as knives and cable-ties, whose beauty lies in their polyvalence. So the trailer became a seat when it was turned upside down, the bike became a clothes horse, and the flagpole a kingpin. The commuter became a pilgrim. It is this exercise of imagination that breeds confidence, and confidence leads to the capacity for adventure. I have never regretted an adventure yet, other than the many I've failed to set out on. A life without adventure is a life not properly lived. That adventure can be physical, or it can be emotional, or it can be intellectual, but it must *be*. In its planning and its execution, and in its digestion and reflection, there is fuel and oil for the machinery of our everyday lives.

Quite simply, I think all of us would be better off if we packed a tent on a bicycle and took off into the wilds from time to time. It is up to each of us to choose what counts as an adventure. For some of us, it will be a day trip, and for others a re-creation of Edinburgh-born John Foster Fraser's two-year-long circumnavigation of the globe at the end of the nineteenth century. And if we aren't confident of being able to plan and execute an adventure then we need to ask ourselves and others why not. This is the stuff of life and if nothing else, time spent in the wilds reveals and amplifies the value of those things that we actually need to live – water, food, shelter, sanitation, fuel and love. All the rest is froth.

* * *

My ride took me over estate roads, forest roads, drove roads, Wade and Caulfield's military roads, Telford's roads, an '80s cycle path and the beds of two disused railways. Each of them was hacked into unforgiving terrain by sheer hard work and always for a good reason – either to tie the Highlands into the southern part of our island or to exploit the resources of the hills.

The abundant rough pasture in the glens produced beef for southern markets and the grazing on the way fuelled their transport over the drove routes. The forests captured sunlight whose energy was stored in timber and released in charcoal burning to produce iron. Forest roads were built to get that wood to the smelter or the saw mill. The military roads were built for two reasons: first, to get soldiers north to suppress rebellion, but equally to transform the society of the Highlands from a clan-based one, where land was parcelled out according to tradition and need, to one based on rent and debt. Telford's roads were built to ease commerce but equally to access the population of the Highlands for military service in the empire. The railways were built to transport timber, whisky and agricultural produce but also to get tourists to the recreational resources of the Highlands and the guns to their estates.

The odd one out in this roll call of economic and social engineering is the cycle path down the side of the dual carriageway leading up to the Drumochter Pass. Of all the ways I followed, it is the outlier, built without any economic plan in mind and cobbled together for pennies from gravel, rubble and disused tarmac. Cycling is big business now, but in the 1980s it was an activity for eccentrics, students and the poor. Yet this short stretch of path beside a road where cycling is technically legal but virtually suicidal now supports cycle touring in the north and is a vital link in the Land's End to John O'Groats cycle industry. And it was only ever created because of a handful of unconventional and persuasive individuals.

We are in the middle of a crisis every bit as threatening to us as the Jacobite rebellions were to the fledgling Union. In the eighteenth century, the threat of revolt drove the construction of our first ever roads fit for wheeled carriages outside of the biggest towns, at a time when the standard agricultural vehicle was a 'slip-cart' dragged on skids. The threats we face now are loneliness, inactivity and loss of contact with the natural world. We are piling up physical and mental health problems. We need to increase our capacity for adventure, risk-taking, self-reliance and our adaptability. Apart from some of the people who own them, no one thinks we should spend less time in our hills and forests. We are much richer now than we were when we wore the drove roads into the hills, dug the military roads in and built the railways. We have the capacity to respond to this crisis and to do it in a way that makes all of our lives richer.

Simple travel through wild, historic places with a goal beyond the destination reset my whole being. What would it take to draw you, fellow citizen, into the idea of crossing our hills by bike?

The answer is a network of rideable paths linking the river basins of the whole country. Planning my journey involved dividing the mainland into river systems and looking along the watersheds between them for rideable paths, then linking those by whatever path, track or road was in the glen below. Imagine what would happen if every glen was connected to its neighbours by rideable trails following the drove roads, footpaths, military roads and disused railways. There is enormous repressed demand for cycle touring. People love our country and they want to visit its wild places in slow, gentle ways, but they are repelled by our noisy, dangerous roads and frightened by the trackless wildernesses they can't access because it's so awkward to get a bike on a train here. The shooting estates that own so much of our land often have a particular brand of welcome that doesn't encourage folk to linger.

The Wade military roads were built quickly in the face of an existential threat to the new country called Great Britain. The first few miles in the Great Glen were as much an experiment in how to make roads in the Highlands as an effort to deliver a final product. They expanded into a national network and, crucially, had Kingshouses or inns for shelter and food, a couple of which still survive as shooting lodges and hotels. We face the threats of inactivity, over-caution and estrangement from nature. Why don't we build a network of simple gravel paths through our hills as a response to this? The work of constructing them would be cheap and healthy, as Wade and Caulfield demonstrated. Rocks and gravel are to hand everywhere and the estate, hydroelectric and wind farm roads are already in place, waiting to be linked up. It isn't difficult to imagine such a network becoming wildly popular in short order. In a couple of years, the North Coast 500, nothing more than a marketing brand for existing tarmac, has become a destination for road cyclists.

The Breadalbane and Grampian hydroelectric schemes took massive efforts in austere times when there was a genuine shortage of materials and food but an abundance of community. People still alive look back on the construction of the dams in the 1950s as the best time of their lives despite the hardship. We live in a time where austerity means the creation of artificial scarcity in an era of material plenty. We can certainly afford to acquire some rough land and revisit techniques from the eighteenth century to build some rock and gravel paths and a few bridges.

We could start with taster paths to see if they are as popular as I'm sure they would be. There's a well-known way across the north-west Highlands from Strath Croe to Beauly that runs through the astonishingly beautiful Glen Affric, at the head of which there is even a youth hostel. Wouldn't people flock to it if the footpath at the western end was upgraded to the type of gravel cycle path that enlightened estates such as Rothiemurchus have built and a way was found to avoid the tarmac roads at the eastern end?

I think many people would be entranced by the idea of a two- or three-day crossing of this wild country. There's a Caulfield-era road that runs from Glen Moriston over to Fort Augustus down a fantastic set of boggy and overgrown switchback bends. The Wade road runs south over the Corrieyairack, and from Feshiebridge there is a way surveyed by Wade but never built over to Braemar.

Why don't we restore the gravel to these military roads to make them rideable again?

We have a huge problem with the dereliction and depopulation of rural areas. Cyclists like to travel light and eat tonnes, so anything that brings them to an area brings money and employment. In addition, they tend to be rugged folk who'll settle for a bunk in a bothy. European countries manage to have mountain refuges with basic meals and beds. Why can't we? Why should the wilderness be the exclusive preserve of extremists like me, willing to drag days of provisions up hill and down dale? Our landscape is an asset for us and for others, and we should be making much more of it.

The major obstacle to such a plan would be the shooting estates. Some have grasped the value of recreational cycling and others have begun the process of letting the trees grow back, but most take the attitude that was made all too clear to me on the many signs I passed. Don't bother us. Slow down. Get off. Get out.

What great wealth has in common with genius is that it allows people to recover their childhood self because it frees them from the limits of everyday life – and the people who own the shooting estates I crossed are all very wealthy. Childhood is a time not just of daydreams and play but also of extreme cruelty, as our ability to hurt outstrips our ability to empathise. I can remember chasing a black beetle around a friend's garden with the laser-beam from a magnifying glass on a sunny day and the acrid smell of the smoke as we cut through its body without a thought for the pain or an ounce of shame. I do wonder if the shooters haven't got their privilege upside down. With a few honourable exceptions they have hills and the freedom to do as they wish with them, but chose a stultifying and codified brand of cruelty to half-tame animals. They cite tradition, dressing in woollen clothes, but while deer have been taken for food for as long as people have been here, the shooting of stags with rifles for trophies is relatively recent; no more than two hundred years, and the whole grouse thing is younger than that. So where they could make themselves forests and genuine wilderness packed with wildlife all year round, they instead drop by in the autumn to engage in a lethal pantomime that strips the hills bare. I've no objection to hunting, as such – I take rabbits for the pot myself – but it seems like such a grim waste of such a privileged position, a failure of the imagination. Some owners of estates seem to have managed to imagine another future for the hills – I just wish the rest of them would take a long and honest look in their gilded mirrors.

Landownership is a vexed subject here and shining too bright a light on it has got people in trouble, not just in the past but as I write. When I camped in Gleann Meurain on the second night, I was on the line of a road from Skye to Edinburgh, surveyed but never built by Thomas Telford at the start of the nineteenth century. It failed not because it wouldn't have been useful, but because, in his words, 'the personal convenience of the proprietors is not immediately concerned'. The estate which this road would have crossed is Auch and Invermearan, the one whose public sub-sidies for 2011 are declared to have been £696,909. Who knows if their personal convenience would be immediately concerned by a gravel track over the pass from Rannoch Moor? Surely the real question is whether they would have any right to object, given the amount of money they have been gifted to maintain the bleak and barren slopes of our hills. The same argument applies to all of the other shooting estates – and in spades to those owned offshore.

A network of gravel tracks passable on a bike with camping gear, studded with refuges in the remote glens, would be good for us, good for local jobs and good for bringing people here to meet us and revel in our land. History has taught us that the construction of lines of communication in the Highlands can be transformative. The military roads allowed wheeled carriages to go where only walkers had ever been before and changed the politics and society of the uplands for good. We don't need roads sixteen feet wide – three feet would be luxury, and one foot would do in places.

If we had the confidence of those who, in the shadow of the Second World War, living on a rationed diet and desperately short of raw materials, built the vast Breadalbane hydroelectric scheme, we could make a start at transforming our nation. The trail centres of the Forestry Commission are good fun, but to me they only emphasise our estrangement from the land outside the playpen and steer folk towards treating cycling in the hills as if it were alpine skiing on wheels – thrilling, dangerous and demanding. What we really need is to slow down and travel through the mountains in a contemplative way.

Pilgrimage has long been a part of our way of life and affected the way we travel. In 1507, James IV made an extraordinary journey from Stirling to Elgin in a day on his way to pray at Tain. The intention was to astonish everyone who witnessed or heard about it. The Queen's ferry across the Forth was as much for pilgrims heading for St Andrews as for trade. It's time we revived that in a modern, secular form and insisted on exercising our rights to roam where we reasonably will, under our own steam and in pursuit of that inner calm that seems so rare and precious.

As I came down from the hills towards the Moray coast, I was treated to displays from two military aircraft: one, a perfectly adequate propeller-driven plane using technology from the 1950s; and the other an American jet so wildly complex that it seems unlikely ever to completely exit the prototype stage before entering obsolescence. Seeing those two machines together made me think about how effective low-technology initiatives can be. The reforested plots on the banks of Loch Garry were the result of a shoestring operation involving some fencing and a handful of seeds. The path down the A9 was cobbled together with spare machinery and found materials. It is perfectly possible to effect real change with modest means, and cycling is the epitome of this philosophy. If we can afford even one of those hopeless jets, we can afford to build a network that allows ordinary people on their ordinary machines to cross the wild watersheds of our land.

When I got to Findhorn, I was possessed by the immediate conviction that my having completed the journey rendered it worthless. If I could do it then, by definition, it wasn't hard enough. Only failure would have provided the necessary affirmation. This feeling – 'the cringe' – is our most powerful enemy, but we must believe that we have the capacity to change our lives or we'll end up, like the makers of Sueno's Stone, erecting monuments to our own defeat. Our most powerful asset is maybe the same one that saw me head for a soaking tent by a river rather than accept the offer of help from a caravan park at Feshiebridge. Standing in a growing puddle, with my shoes and pockets full of water as the nervous bourgeoisie looked anxiously on in the bar of the water sports centre, I felt a deep sense of humiliation. That's what steeled my resolve not to take any easy options but to stick to my plan, and it's the same feeling I get looking at our cramped lives and the vast spaces given over to the cruel amusements of a tiny few.

Whether it is on a national network of brand new wilderness cycle paths or on the multitude of stalkers' paths, estate and windfarm roads that are already there for us, let's get out there. Life is short and the active part of it can be shorter still. If you want to follow my trail, go right ahead, but there are an infinity of others just waiting. Cyclists dismount? No. Cyclists mount. Turn the cranks over.

Bibliography

Anderson, M.L., *A History of Scottish Forestry* (Nelson, 1967)

Devine, T.M., Lee, C.H., and Peden, G.C. (editors), *The Transformation of Scotland: The Economy Since 1700* (Edinburgh University Press, 2005)

Galbraith, Russell, *Without Quarter: A Biography of Tom Johnston* (Mainstream, 1995)

Geddes, Patrick, 'Nature Study and Geographical Education', *The Scottish Geographical Magazine*, October 1902

Gordon, Seton, *Highways and Byways in the Central Highlands* (MacMillan, 1949)

Grant, Elspeth, *Abernethy Forest: Its People and Its Past* (The Arkleton Trust, 1994)

Haldane, A.R.B., *The Drove Roads of Scotland* (David & Charles, 1952)

Haldane, A.R.B., *New Ways Through the Glens* (Thomas Nelson & Sons, 1962)

Hendry, George, *Midges in Scotland* (Aberdeen University Press, 1989)

Inglis, Harry R.G., *The 'Contour' Road Book of Scotland* (Gall and Inglis, 1901)

McConnochie, Alexander Inkson, *The Deer and Deer Forests of Scotland* (H.F. & G. Witherby, 1923)

McKane, Phil, *Scotland Mountain Biking: The Wild Trails* (Vertebrate, 2009)

Payne, Peter L., *The Hydro* (Aberdeen University Press, 1988)

Richards, Eric, *A History of the Highland Clearances* (Croom Helm, 1982)

Robinson, Mairi (editor-in-chief), *The Concise Scots Dictionary* (Aberdeen University Press, 1985)

Roy, William, *The Great Map: The Military Survey of Scotland 1747–55* (Birlinn, 2007)

Salmond, J.B., *Wade in Scotland* (The Moray Press, 1938)

Shepherd, Nan, *The Living Mountain* (Aberdeen University Press, 1977)

Smout, T.C., Macdonald, Alan R., and Watson, Fiona, *A History of the Native Woodlands of Scotland 1500–1920* (Edinburgh University Press, 2004)

Southwick, Leslie, *The So-Called Sueno's Stone at Forres* (Moray District Library, 1981)

Sutherland, Elizabeth, *The Pictish Guide* (Birlinn, 1997)

Taylor, William, *The Military Roads in Scotland* (House of Lochar, 1996)

Thomas, John, *Forgotten Railways: Scotland* (David & Charles, 1976)

Vallance, H.A., *The Great North of Scotland Railway* (David St John Thomas, 1965)

Veitch, Kenneth, *et al* (editors), *Scottish Life and Society: A Compendium of Scottish Ethnology, Volume Eight: Transport and Communications* (John Donald, 2009)

Wightman, Andy, *Who Owns Scotland* (Canongate Books, 1996)

Wood, Emma, *The Hydro Boys – Pioneers of Renewable Energy* (Luath, 2002)

Yeoman, Peter, *Pilgrimage in Medieval Scotland* (B.T. Batsford, 1999)

Acknowledgements

Writing a book is a laborious journey that doesn't make the author any better company than they were before they set out on it. This work was only possible because of the tolerance, forbearance, encouragement, and love of my partner, Nathalie. She has my most heartfelt thanks.

It takes a certain audacity to believe that you can write something worth the reading, and I would never have thought myself capable of it without the help of a whole village.

My biology tutor at university, Geoff Harper, was the best English teacher I had. He trusted us to teach ourselves biology, while he taught us to think, write and talk. Sally Hinchcliffe's spontaneous kindness about something I wrote online gave me pause for thought. I'm grateful to both Duncan Hothersall and Stuart Campbell for publishing essays of mine on their websites. Lisa Ballantyne told me how to write the first line of this book and Jamie Reed-Baxter told me how to reach the last one. Peggy Hughes took me through the daunting process of finding a publisher. Sara Hunt at Saraband saw something in the text others had not, and Craig Hillsley carved an actual book out of the pile of words in my laptop, whilst Jei Degenhardt proofread it diligently.

I got to thinking more deeply about cycling, and what it means, through engaging with the CityCyclingEdinburgh.info forum community. Many members there have contributed something to this book, including DrAfternoon, Slug, DaveC, cb, kaputnik and

Morningsider. Cyclingmollie lent me his Edwardian cycling guide without our ever having met before. It's that kind of place.

Many others also made this thing possible, particularly my test readers, Ewen Maclean – who both introduced me to Peggy and pushed me just when I needed it – Fi Riddick, Alan Ritchie and my brother, Phil. John Grimshaw and Dave Holladay gave me the inside track on the A9 cycle path. Alfie Noakes chummed me over my first coast-to-coast. Audrey Neill was better for me than I was for myself. Andy Wightman pointed me to the Registers of Scotland's online land ownership search facility. The unfailing warmth and courtesy of the National Library of Scotland's staff should be a lesson to the other national archives. There will be others I've forgotten – you have my thanks too.

Finally, by way of disclaimer, I should add that the conversations contained in this book are described to the best of my ability – they may not be verbatim but each is recounted as fairly and accurately as my notes and memory allow.

About the author

Born and brought up in Aberdeen, Alan left to study environmental and then physical chemistry in Edinburgh, spurred on by a desire to know the particular workings of the world. He then worked as a research chemist, and later translator, in France for a few years where he developed a lifelong passion for the country's language, culture and literature. Having initially sought refuge from the instabilities of academic life in Edinburgh's financial and cultural institutions he then became a freelance programmer, analyst and change manager before giving in to the urge to write. The place of bicycles in a mentally and physically healthy life and in the circular economy of liveable cities is another enduring passion, and *Overlander*, his first published work, is in part an attempt to express the deep joy that can come from cycling an ordinary bike over any terrain, but especially through our hills and forests.

e-mail: overlanderthebook@gmail.com
Twitter: @overlanderb1